the MEAT, POULTRY & GAME COOKBOOK

the MEAT, POULTRY & GAME COOKBOOK

CONSULTANT EDITOR

Sarah Banbery

p

This is a Parragon Publishing Book
First published in 2006

Parragon Publishing
Queen Street House
4 Queen Street
Bath BA1 1HE, UK

ISBN: 1-40548-037-8

Printed in Thailand

Created and produced by:
The Bridgewater Book Company Ltd

Commissioned photography Clive Bozzard-Hill
Home economist Sandra Baddeley
Photography (front cover) Mike Cooper
Home economist (front cover) Sumi Glass
Illustrations Coral Mula

The Bridgewater Book Company would like to thank the following for permission to reproduce copyright material: Frank Herholdt/Taxi/Getty Images, page 10; Owen Franken/Corbis, page 11; George D. Lepp/Corbis, page 22; and Murat Taner/zefa/Corbis, page 23.

Notes for the Reader

This book uses imperial, metric, and US cup measurements. Follow the same units of measurement throughout; do not mix imperial and metric. All spoon measurements are level: teaspoons are assumed to be 5 ml, and tablespoons are assumed to be 15 ml. Unless otherwise stated, milk is assumed to be whole, eggs and individual vegetables are medium, and pepper is freshly ground black pepper. Recipes using raw or very lightly cooked eggs should be avoided by infants, the elderly, pregnant women, convalescents, and anyone suffering from an illness. Pregnant and breastfeeding women are advised to avoid eating peanuts and peanut products.

CONTENTS

INTRODUCTION

1

The Meat, Poultry, and Game Cookbook is a comprehensive guide to choosing, buying, storing, and cooking meat, whether it be red meat, poultry, or game. If you find yourself struggling to identify the bewildering variety of cuts of meat available, or if you want to know the best way to cook different types of poultry, then here you will find all the information you need in a single volume. From finding new uses for familiar meats to preparing more unusual and hard-to-find game, this book will give you not only the confidence to select the appropriate and best produce, but also a wealth of both traditional and contemporary ways to cook and serve it, drawn from culinary traditions across the globe.

INTRODUCTION

There are many kinds of meat, and different cultures may favor or avoid eating certain species, but in the Western world, "meat" means common farmed or wild mammals and birds. The majority of us are meat-eaters, but often look no further than a pack of ground meat or a pork chop to satisfy our appetites and taste buds. This book aims to inject a new spirit of excitement into your kitchen by helping you to explore the myriad tastes and textures of various types of meat, to make your cooking more creative, adventurous, and delicious.

Eating meat may not, strictly speaking, be essential for our survival but it is nutritionally important and tastes good. The huge variety of recipes in this book demonstrates meat's versatility and popularity throughout the world as the basis for a nutritious, delicious meal for the whole family. For those who find it difficult to know where to start, read through this chapter for guidance on selecting and storing the most common types of meat, whether it be red meat, poultry, or game. There is a section on how to prepare your produce for cooking and details on how to cook and carve meat. This book will also help you to identify good meat. Always buy the best produce on offer and don't be tempted to go for poor quality, mass-produced meat. It is far better to buy smaller amounts or cheaper cuts of good meat rather than large amounts of bad. Apart from the ethical considerations of industrially produced meat, and the nutritional value of the product, the difference in taste, for example, between free-range chickens and their factory-farmed counterparts is noticeable. Once you have developed a taste for good, fresh meat, you'll never want to eat poor-quality meat again!

CHOOSING MEAT, POULTRY, AND GAME

To take advantage of the huge variety of meat, poultry, and game available, including cured, preserved, and processed meats as well as variety meats, it is useful to have a basic understanding of what is on offer in its various forms.

MEAT

Terms applied to different varieties of a particular meat, such as lamb, are often related to the age of the animal. It is worth bearing in mind that the meat of younger animals is generally more tender, but also less pronounced in flavor, while older animals are likely to be tougher yet tastier.

BEEF AND VEAL

Beef is the meat provided by domestic cattle, while veal is the meat of the young calf. Beef usually comes from castrated male cattle slaughtered at between 18 and 24 months and veal from male calves slaughtered at either three weeks, 18–20 weeks or between five and six months. There are many types of beef produced from a large number of different types of cattle, including: "dairy cross" meat produced from the offspring of a dairy cow and a bull, "prime beef" from a pedigree herd, "rare" beef, from rare breeds, or prized "kobe beef," which comes from Wagyu cattle.

HALAL AND KOSHER MEAT AND POULTRY

These types of meat and poultry are raised according to religious law and ritually slaughtered by a specialist butcher with a razor-sharp knife. They are available from specialist butchers and some supermarkets.

LAMB AND MUTTON

Lamb is the meat from a young sheep, and there are several types:

Baby Lamb/Suckling: milk-fed lamb no older than ten weeks and weighing less than 20 lb/9.1 kg.

Spring Lamb: several months old and 20–40 lb/9.1–18 kg.

Lamb: five months to one year old and most commonly available.

Hogget/Yearling: meat from a lamb that is one to two years old.

Mutton: meat of a mature sheep over two years old.

PORK, HAM, AND BACON

Pork is the fresh meat of the domestic pig. Traditionally, pork was seasonal meat, much of which was salted and preserved to provide ham, bacon, and sausages. Most pork is slaughtered between six and nine months old, and anything older is termed a "hog." "Rare-breed" pork is almost exclusively free-range.

VARIETY MEATS

The term "variety meats" refers to the edible parts of an animal left over when the meat is removed from the carcass. This includes organs such as the heart, liver, and kidneys as well as tongue, brain, thymus gland (sweetbreads), stomach lining (tripe), and blood (used in blood sausage). The term also covers pig's feet, head and jowl, ox tail, and calf's trotter.

POULTRY

Poultry is defined as domestic fowl bred specifically for eating. Raised for their meat and eggs, poultry includes chicken, turkey, duck, goose, and guinea fowl.

CHICKEN

This is the most widely available form of poultry, and also the most popular. Chicken is sold under a number of different names according to its age, size, and method of rearing. The following are the most common types of chicken you are likely to come across:

Squab Chicken: an immature chicken, four to six weeks old, weighing up to 1 lb/450 g with delicate, moist meat.

Spring Chicken: a small, young bird weighing up to 2 lb 8 oz/1.15 kg.

Broiler or Roasting Chicken: the most common bird for roasting, a full-sized bird weighs between 3–6 lb/1.3–2.7 kg.

Boiling Fowl/Stewing Chicken: an older bird, usually a laying hen weighing 6 lb/2.7 kg.

Capon: a castrated young chicken bred for its tender, white flesh.

Corn Fed: chickens fed on corn, which produces a yellow flesh and skin with a flavor comparable to guinea fowl.

Free Range: indicates that a limited number of birds are housed per

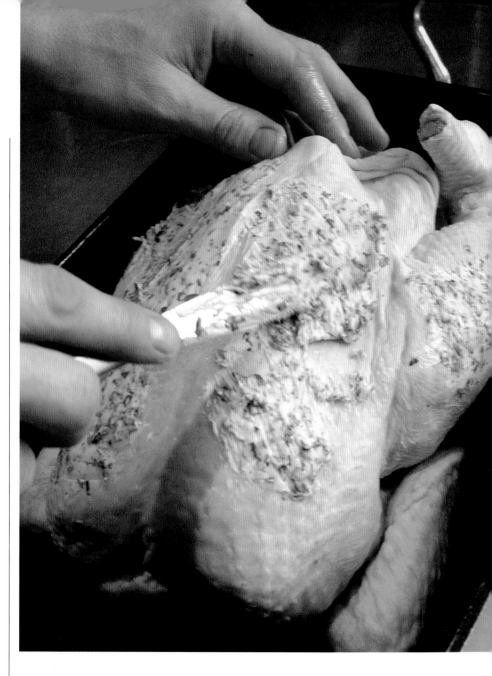

square yard/meter and have outside access for at least half their life.

Traditional Free Range: indicates chickens that have more space and must have had outside access from the age of six weeks.

Free Range–Total Freedom: this is very similar to traditional free range, except that during daylight hours, outside access is unrestricted.

Battery: intensively reared chickens with no outside access, killed at six weeks old.

Organic: chickens raised with a regulated standard of welfare, that are GM-free and have been fed with antibiotic-free food and with guaranteed access to forage and feed outside.

GUINEA FOWL

Originally game birds, guinea fowl are now almost exclusively farmed. Slightly smaller than chickens when plucked, guinea fowl are sold as squabs weighing 1 lb 4 oz/550 g, chicks weighing up to 2 lb 4 oz/1 kg, or fowls weighing up to 3 lb 12 oz/1.7 kg. The hen bird is considered to be the more tender.

TURKEY

Descended from the North American wild turkey, this domestic bird is available all year round. A young turkey weighing 8–24 lb/3.6–11 kg will provide about 70 percent white meat and 30 percent dark meat. Allow an average of 12 oz/350 g per person. The rearing methods for turkeys are similar to chickens, so an organic, free-range bird will have a better flavor and texture than an intensively raised bird.

READY-PREPARED CHICKEN CUTS

You can purchase chicken in a variety of forms to save on preparation time, including: chicken quarters; part-boned or boneless breast; drumsticks (legs); thighs and wings.

DUCK AND GOOSE

Duck is a waterfowl, now mainly raised commercially and widely available. There are a number of varieties, and as with all poultry, a younger, free-range bird will taste better than an older, farmed bird.

Most duck on offer is actually duckling, which is typically six to eight weeks old, but duck up to 16 weeks old is sometimes sold. A 6-lb/2.7-kg duck will feed two or three people.

Goose is a large water bird that is popular for roasting and is raised free-range. Fatty and with rich meat, it has an average weight of 6–12 lb/ 2.7–5.4 kg, but because of its meat-to-fat ratio, a goose will only feed four people, on average.

GAME

Strictly speaking, "game" is defined as birds and mammals that are wild and hunted for the table. Traditionally, game has been a seasonal food, usually available for a short period of time, and from wild animals and birds shot for the pot and sold through a game dealer. However, today very little game is truly wild, and it is available for most of the year. Farmed, frozen, or imported game birds and animals may well have lived part of their life "wild," but have nevertheless been reared specifically for supplying to supermarkets and butchers. More unusual game is now available by mail order from specialist game dealers. It is useful when buying game birds to know if they are young birds, which will roast well, or older birds that will need to be braised or stewed for the best results. Game is traditionally "hung" to develop flavor.

PHEASANT

The pheasant is a long-tailed game bird originally from China and related to the chicken, available farmed or as wild game birds. Traditionally, a "brace," or a male and female pair of birds, is cooked at one time, the smaller hen bird being regarded as the most juicy and tender. Pheasant tend to be very lean with a strong, rich flavor and are best enjoyed roasted or braised. Wild birds are in season from October to February, but fresh, farmed birds are available generally from September to March. One pheasant will feed two people. Keep refrigerated for two days—any longer and the birds will acquire a very strong "gamey" smell and taste.

GROUSE

Grouse are a family of sought-after wild game birds, which includes the sage grouse, capercaillie, and the red grouse. Fairly lean and with a distinctive flavor, the grouse is only found wild. A good bird can be distinguished by its plump breast and unblemished skin. Older birds should be casseroled or braised rather than roasted. Available from August/September, one bird is usually served per person and they can be hung for up to ten days, depending on how strong a flavor you desire.

PARTRIDGE

A small, plump, flavorsome game bird, the best-known partridge are the red-legged and the gray-legged. Farmed partridge tend to have less

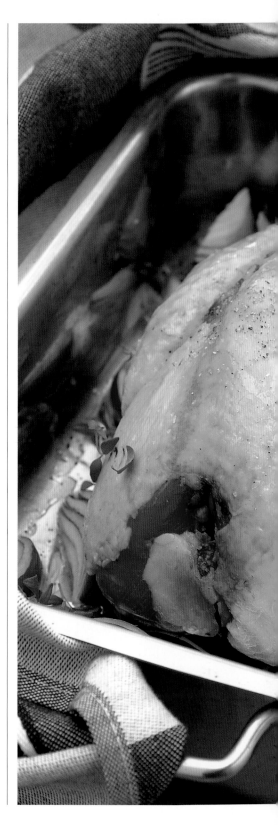

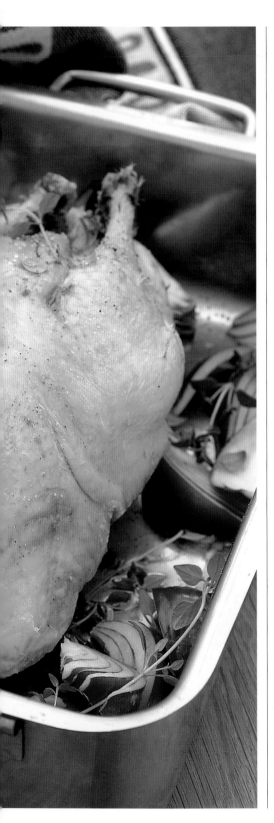

taste than their wild counterparts, but the meat of both is very lean and highly flavored. Related to the pheasant, partridge have a slightly firmer flesh and should be prepared and cooked in a similar way. One bird is usually served per person.

QUAIL

A small game bird related to the pheasant and partridge, quail are available almost exclusively farmed. The quail has a pink, moist flesh when cooked, and due to its limited size, it is usual to serve two per person as a main dish. Available all year round, the quail is also prized for its tiny eggs, traditionally used in canapés. Often prepared part-boned for stuffing, quail can also be spatchcocked.

WOODCOCK AND SNIPE

Both woodcock and snipe are rare and highly prized wild birds, sought after for their dark, intense meat. As they are difficult to shoot, they are not generally available, although they can occasionally be acquired from a good game dealer or direct from a shoot. They do not generally improve with age, so should be cooked within a week of obtaining them. Traditionally, the woodcock, and sometimes snipe, are cooked

whole (with their intestines), including the head. Allow one bird per person.

PIGEON AND SQUAB

Pigeon are common game birds and there are hundreds of species worldwide. A squab is a young, domestic pigeon that has never flown. Pigeon flesh is dark, rich, and dense, with very firm flesh on the breast, while squab tends to be more succulent and pink. Widely available, pigeon is best cooked as fresh as possible and the breasts are often pan-fried or roasted; older birds require slow cooking.

WILD DUCK

Mallard, a type of wild duck, are raised semi-wild specifically for shooting. They have lean, dry flesh and should only be hung for one day. One bird will serve two people.

WILD TURKEYS

Native to North America, the turkey has been domesticated and exported worldwide, but wild turkeys are still regarded as game birds. Among the largest game birds, they live in flocks and are leaner than a domestic turkey, with dark, dense meat.

VENISON

Venison is defined as "large antlered game" and therefore, as well as deer, it includes elk, caribou, moose, antelope, bison, and buffalo. Venison is still mainly sourced from deer, and until farmed venison became widely available, it was seasonal, expensive meat. Venison is lean, close-textured, dark, moist meat, with a pronounced gamey flavor. All venison animals are similar in taste and texture, and the same cooking methods apply. The best deer venison comes from a young buck deer aged up to two years. Broadly, the meat can be treated in the same way as beef, although it is leaner and therefore often needs the addition of pork fat to keep it moist. Prime roasting joints tend to come from the leg (haunch), the loin, and the saddle, while the boned loin provides steaks.

The rest of the meat can be used in different ways, including being casseroled, made into sausages, or ground.

HANGING MEAT

Hanging a carcass or part of a carcass, literally from a hook, ages or matures it. The process allows the muscle to relax and tenderize, and to lose moisture, which means that the meat is less likely to shrink or dry out when cooking. All meat should be hung for a few days, and mature beef, mutton, venison and other game benefit from longer hanging to allow the flavor to develop.

RABBIT

Available both farmed and wild, rabbit is an inexpensive, lowfat meat. Wild rabbit is considered to have a more pronounced flavor than farmed. Rabbit meat is pale and fine-grained with a delicate flavor, and although available year round, the "season" for the best-quality rabbit is August to February. Rabbit is usually eaten at three months old, and one rabbit will feed two people.

HARE

Larger than a rabbit, with long back legs, the hare is almost exclusively available from game dealers. The meat is rich, moist, and has a distinctive flavor. As with other game, young hare is best roasted or "jugged"—marinated, casseroled with vegetables and served in a sauce enriched with the hare's blood and liver, and cream. Older hare should be casseroled or only the saddle roasted. One hare should feed two or three people.

WILD BOAR

A traditional European game animal, the wild boar is a wild pig that has distinctive dark, rich, close-grained meat, which contains much less fat than domestic pork. Until recently almost exclusively wild meat, boar are now being farm-raised and have increased in popularity for "hog roasts" and as sausages. Boar is butchered in the same manner as pork and the most tender cuts come from the loin. Boar should always be cooked well done.

BACON

This is cured back and belly pork. Bacon can be either wet-cured in salted water or dry-cured, where salt or a mixture of salt, sugar, and spices are rubbed into the pork. The meat can then be smoked.

HAM

The hind leg of the pig is salted and air-dried or brined and smoked to make ham. There are a number of curing methods that involve a variety of seasonings, spices, and sugar, and may include such flavorings as molasses, beer, and red wine.

SALT BEEF

Dry-cured brisket or silverside beef is known as salt beef. The longer the meat spends in the salt or brine defines how salty the final meat will taste, and the longer it is cured, the longer it will last, but it may well have to be soaked before cooking.

AIR-DRIED MEATS

Air-drying is a further maturing process for cured meat—once cured, the meat is hung and left to dry and develop further. Most air-dried meats, including air-dried sausage (salami) and prosciutto and serrano ham, are then eaten raw.

SALAMIS

These air-dried, cured sausages use natural casings made from preserved and reconstituted animal intestines, which are pliable for stuffing with meat.

CURED, PRESERVED, AND PROCESSED MEATS

"Curing" simply means preserving by various age-old methods of salting, pickling, air-drying, wind-drying, and smoking, or otherwise treating meat and offal to ensure that it will last longer than fresh meat. Processed meats include pâtés, terrines, potted meats, and pies.

COLD-SMOKED MEATS

Cold-smoking is another method of preserving and flavoring meat, once again applied to ready-cured meat. The meat is hung over smoking coals or woodchips, which further reduces the moisture content of the meat and adds preservatives. Most, but not all, cold-smoked meat needs cooking.

CONFIT

In this traditional method of preserving, the meat is initially dry-salted—sometimes spiced—and then cooked for a long time in rendered fat until very soft, poured into a jar, and completely covered in liquid fat, which solidifies and preserves the meat for up to six months. This is a popular method for preserving duck, goose, rabbit, and pork.

SAUSAGES

Fresh sausages are made by blending lean, chopped meat and fat with seasoning and spices, herbs, and cereal or rusk. Most meat, game, and poultry are now available in sausages, including duck, venison, and wild boar. The meat content of sausages varies greatly and there are some varieties of sausage, such as blood sausage, that are made without meat. The best sausages have a high meat content with a good amount of pork fat to keep them moist, with well-balanced flavorings, and natural casings. Good sausages should not be pricked before cooking, as this lets the fat that keeps them moist leach out.

PIES

Pork or other pork-based picnic pies, including game pies, are really terrines, where pastry replaces the dish. The pastry surrounding the chopped meat should be a shortening-rich, hot watercrust pastry. Pies, which can include veal, poultry, and game, can keep fresh for up to a month.

PÂTÉS AND TERRINES

Pâté is distinct from a terrine in that terrines tend to have larger pieces of meat and/or vegetable, whereas a pâté is either a smooth paste or has a coarse chopped-meat texture. Liver is often the basis of a pâté (pork or chicken), with the addition of chopped pork. Goose liver pâté is the most luxurious. Game also works well in pâtés and terrines because of its strong, distinctive flavors. Both pâtés and terrines are a traditional way of using up leftover meat or variety meats and can be made of virtually any pieces of meat, poultry, or game, including sweetbreads.

BUYING MEAT, POULTRY, AND GAME

Nowadays there are various ways in which you can buy meat, poultry, and game, and where you buy your meat can affect not only what you buy in terms of availability but also quality. As well as being discriminating as to sourcing your produce, it is well worth learning how to detect the signs of well-produced and processed meat, poultry, and game. While it is unnecessary to know every cut of meat and where it comes from, it is useful to understand broadly what you need to buy for your intended purpose and the end result you want.

WHERE TO BUY

The usual sources include supermarkets, butchers, markets, farm shops and producers, a game supplier, or straight from the wild. Many people are becoming more interested in where their meat comes from and will spend time sourcing meat from a particular supplier to satisfy their own concerns regarding welfare and nutrition.

SUPERMARKETS

A majority of the meat we buy still comes from supermarkets and they have the advantage of huge buying power. They also offer convenience both in terms of long opening hours and ready-prepared produce, as well as a guarantee of freshness. The labeling of supermarket goods gives the consumer some information on sourcing of products, and in recent years more effort has been made to raise the standards of animal welfare.

GAME SUPPLIERS AND WILD SOURCES

Many game birds and animals are now available from supermarkets and specialist butchers, but traditionally, it was the game suppliers who provided wild game shot by a local shoot. This is still the case, and buying game through a traditional supplier is the only way of guaranteeing freshness and indeed having the opportunity to hang your own game and prepare it at home.

THE INTERNET

Meat is increasingly available by mail order from suppliers via the Internet, and many supermarkets now provide shopping on-line for home delivery. The Internet is also a good way of investigating farmers' markets and local producers. Rare or unusual meat, such as ostrich and buffalo, can usually be sourced from specialist suppliers and there is also information on offer regarding animal welfare and organic standards, as well as recipes.

BUTCHERS

A good local butcher should offer a wide choice and be knowledgeable with regard to the provenance of the produce, be able to order and prepare special cuts of meat for you, and generally offer reliable advice when you are making a purchase. You are also likely to find the more traditional and unusual cuts of meat and game from a butcher. He or she should also know how long meat or game has been hung.

MARKETS, FARM SHOPS, AND DIRECT SALES FROM PRODUCERS

Those who are concerned with animal welfare and traceability will more often source meat, poultry, and game direct from producers or via a market or farm shop. Dealing direct with the producer means that the consumer can be satisfied as to the way in which the meat has been raised, transported, and slaughtered.

WHAT TO LOOK FOR

Once you begin to understand what to look for when choosing meat, poultry, or game, the whole process of cooking becomes easier, as you are likely to have selected the best-quality meat for your dish.

BEEF AND VEAL

Avoid bright pink/cerise meat with very little fat, as this indicates that the meat has not been properly hung and is likely to lack flavor—well-hung beef will have a deep color and flavor. Good-quality beef should be deep red, dry, and with a sheen (not wet or sweating), and slightly tacky to the touch. The meat should be open-grained, have good marbling (see opposite), and a significant amount of creamy fat—the fat should not be yellow or gray, and any beef with a pink/brown two-toned color or unpleasant smell should be avoided. Veal should be a delicate pale pink color with very little fat.

LAMB

The flesh should be light red in color, moist, and have a layer of firm, creamy fat. A good-quality lamb joint should have fresh, plump flesh, a significant layer of fat, and pliable skin. Avoid any lamb with yellowing fat or graying flesh that has a strong smell.

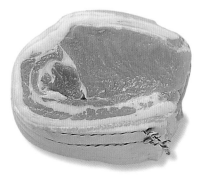

PORK

The flesh should be pale pink, smooth, and fine-grained, with a visible moist sheen, while the fat should be creamy, pale, firm, and have a pliable, smooth rind. The rind is a good indicator of freshness and should be thin, pinkish, and flexible. Avoid any pork with a rubbery, thick or brown rind with any hair.

CHICKEN AND TURKEY

Birds should have plump breasts, white flesh under unblemished skin, and the legs should be pliable with taut skin. The skin should be a pale white/cream and the bird should not be wet or leaking blood. Corn-fed chicken will have a yellow flesh and skin.

DUCK AND GOOSE

Duck has darker meat than chicken and a greater proportion of fat. Look out for long, plump breasts with unblemished skin—the skin should be pale, creamy, and dry. The legs should be flexible and have a good layer of fat under the skin. Like duck, goose should be plump, with a good fatty layer and pale, unblemished skin.

GUINEA FOWL

Guinea fowl should look like a cross between a chicken and a pheasant, with a plump breast and creamy, dry skin.

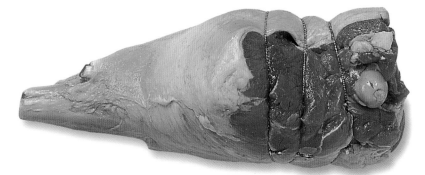

CHOOSING CHECKPOINTS

When making your selection of produce, you should carry out the following checks:

- Meat should not be wet or flabby: It should be shiny, firm, and tacky to the touch. Avoid meat swimming in blood or bloody water.

- Smell it: Fresh meat and poultry does not smell strongly, and only well-hung meat or game should have a distinctive "gamey" smell.

- Chicken should be pale and supple: Avoid any chicken with stained skin or dryness around the edges.

- Check the color of fat on meat: It should be opaque and creamy. Avoid any fat that is yellow or brown.

- Look for good marbling in joints of meat (see below right).

GAME BIRDS

If you can obtain game birds unplucked, it is easier to establish their freshness. A soft, flexible bill and claws indicate a young bird, while a harder, less-flexible bill and ragged claws are the features of an older bird. It is more difficult to establish freshness if you have an oven-ready

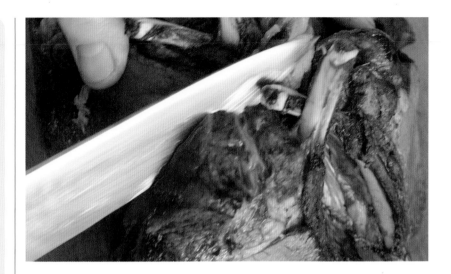

bird, but in general, a soft, flexible breastbone and plump breast indicates a youngster. Game birds should be hung, but an overpoweringly "gamey" smell may indicate a bird that is past its best. Because game is hung intact, unlike beef and lamb, temperature has a crucial effect on how long the bird should be hung, and this really is a case of following your nose—the stronger the smell, the stronger the bird will taste.

VENISON AND WILD BOAR

Venison meat should have a dark, burgundy red appearance with very little fat. Moist and close-textured, it should be firm to the touch, lean, and juicy. Wild boar also has dark meat, but resembles pork more closely, except that is has less fat. Boar has dense, close-textured meat.

RABBIT AND HARE

They should be well covered in flesh, with a rounded back. The flesh should be pale pink, dry, and with a sheen. Pure white fat should be present around the kidneys.

MARBLING IN MEAT

"Marbling" is a reliable indicator of the quality of meat. Marbling is the term for the network of fine fat threaded throughout the flesh, which melts and bastes the meat as it cooks, keeping it moist and tender. It is most obvious in beef, but can also be detected in pork and mutton.

CHOOSING THE RIGHT CUT

It really is essential that you choose and buy the appropriate piece of meat for a particular cooking method. Even the cheapest cut of meat, such as a beef short plate or oxtail, will benefit from the right treatment—marinating and then slow cooking is a foolproof way of dealing with what might otherwise be a tough piece of meat. Always check the recipe or with your supplier that you are using the right cut of meat—if in doubt, order the cut or bird you need in advance. You can usually arrange for your meat or bird to be prepared ready for your dish if you plan ahead. Don't feel you have to struggle to de-bone or otherwise prepare your meat when a butcher can usually do all the hard work for you.

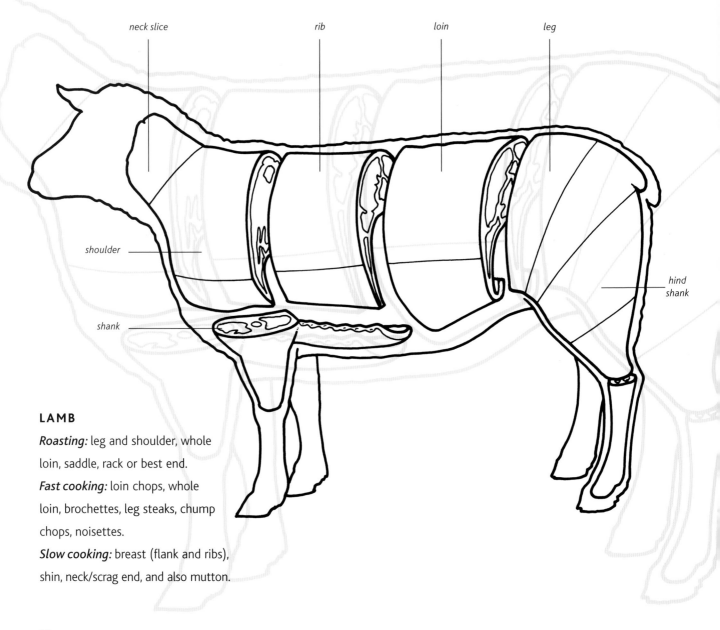

neck slice   rib   loin   leg

shoulder

hind shank

shank

LAMB

Roasting: leg and shoulder, whole loin, saddle, rack or best end.
Fast cooking: loin chops, whole loin, brochettes, leg steaks, chump chops, noisettes.
Slow cooking: breast (flank and ribs), shin, neck/scrag end, and also mutton.

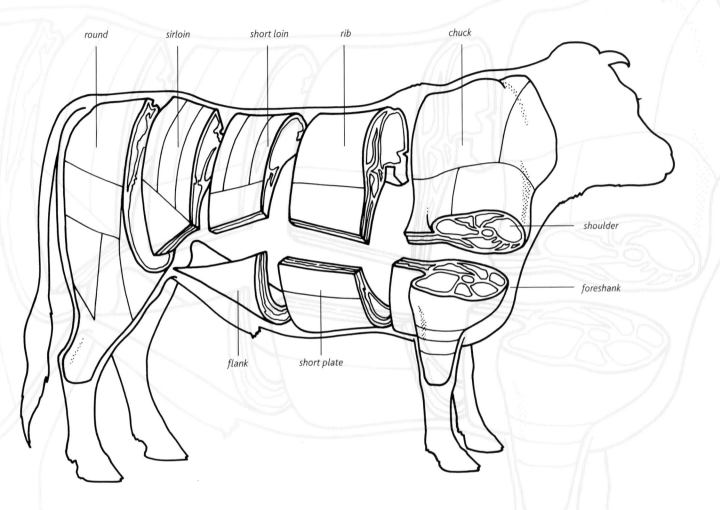

round   sirloin   short loin   rib   chuck

shoulder

foreshank

flank   short plate

BEEF

Roasting: sirloin joint, double-rib joint, wing rib, back rib.

Fast cooking: prime beef steak or tenderloin (filet mignon/ tournedos), sirloin steak, rump steak, T-bone steak, rib-eye steak.

Slow cooking: forequarter meat, such as chuck or blade, chuck steak, short plate, oxtail, leg or hock, shin, silverside, short ribs, brisket.

VEAL

Roasting: round (cushion), loin, chump end or fillet roast, shoulder.

Fast cooking: escalopes, veal chops.

Slow cooking: breast (flank and ribs), shin, neck/scrag end.

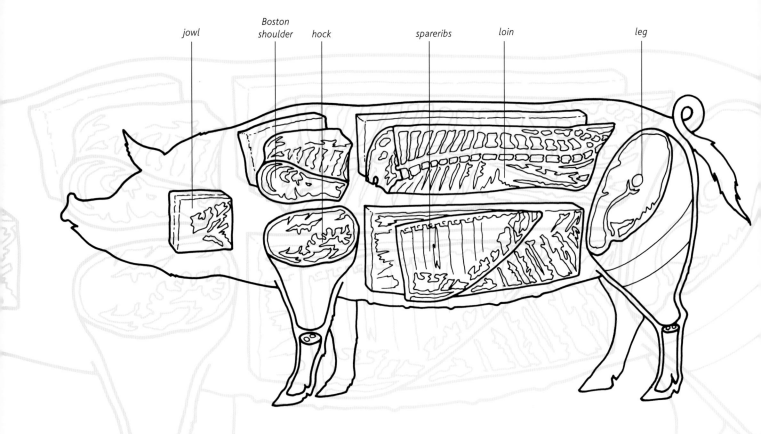

jowl · Boston shoulder · hock · spareribs · loin · leg

PORK

Roasting: leg, loin or sparerib, tenderloin, belly (side pork).

Fast cooking: tenderloin, chops, escalopes, leg steaks, bacon.

Slow cooking: bacon joint, ham, shoulder, knuckle of bacon.

POULTRY

Roasting: chicken, duck, goose, turkey, guinea fowl.

Fast cooking: chicken breasts.

GAME

Roasting: young game birds, venison (saddle and leg), young rabbit.

Fast cooking: venison steaks, pigeon breasts, pheasant breasts.

Slow cooking: older game birds, venison, rabbit, hare.

STORING AND HANDLING MEAT, POULTRY, AND GAME

It is vitally important to store and handle meat, poultry, and game safely to prevent any bacteria that may be present from spreading and causing food poisoning.

HANDLING

• Always wash your hands after handling raw meat, poultry, or game.
• Thoroughly clean all boards, utensils, surfaces, and knives with boiling water when they have been in contact with raw or thawed meat.
• Keep a separate cutting board for preparing meat and poultry, and make sure that it is always scrupulously clean.

STORING

Be sure to follow these guidelines to ensure a high standard of food hygiene and safety:

• Store raw meat or poultry in clean, sealed containers on the bottom shelf of the refrigerator, so that it cannot touch or drip onto other food.
• Follow any storage instructions on labels and do not exceed the "use by" date.
• Store cooked meat in the refrigerator or freezer as soon as it has cooled. Always keep cooked meat and raw meat separate.
• Larger game or turkey can be kept outside, well wrapped in a secure place, with the temperature not exceeding 46°F/8°C.
• Vacuum packing is not good for meat, as it tends to make it sweat, so remove any produce from the pack and either store in a sealed container in the refrigerator or put onto a plate covered with a clean dish towel in the refrigerator.

• Do not keep fresh meat for longer than two days.
• Fresh ground meat and variety meats should be used on the day of purchase where possible.

FREEZING

It is safe to freeze raw meat, poultry, and game as long as you follow these guidelines:

• Freeze any meat before its "use by" date.
• Follow any freezing and thawing instructions on the label.
• Thaw in a microwave only when the meat is to be cooked straight away, otherwise leave in the refrigerator until thoroughly thawed.
• Use thawed meat within two days of thawing.
• Always cook thawed produce thoroughly and until piping hot.
• Raw meat that has been thawed and cooked may then be refrozen, but only once.
• Liquid can appear when meat is thawing and this must not come into contact with other food, so keep in a sealed container and drain regularly.
• Poultry must be thoroughly thawed, but never attempt to speed up the thawing process of this or any other meat by using hot water.

FREEZING GAME BIRDS

If you wish to freeze game, make sure it is hung to your satisfaction and plucked, drawn, and ready to cook. Wipe any excess blood from the carcass. Wrap it in paper, put in a freezer bag, seal, and freeze. Thaw thoroughly and cook as usual, bearing in mind that the freezing process may render the flesh slightly drier than that of a fresh bird. Frozen game can also be cubed and frozen, then thawed to make a game casserole or pie.

PREPARING MEAT, POULTRY, AND GAME

How you prepare your produce for cooking has a major bearing on the end result. There are various ways in which you can enhance its flavor and ensure succulence. Whole chickens or turkeys are mostly sold ready prepared for roasting, usually without giblets. But you may want to divide up a whole bird into separate pieces to make it more manageable for cooking. Knowing how to bone a bird is also a useful technique.

MARINADES AND DRY RUBS

Most meat benefits from seasoning before cooking, but do not overdo the salt—it is better to add salt near the end of cooking, as it can leach juices from the meat. Garlic, herbs, and flavored butter can all enhance the taste of meat, poultry, and game, and a marinade or dry rub will also add character. A marinade is simply a wet flavoring and an easy way of adding taste. It may also help to tenderize some cuts of meat and game. Avoid marinades that are excessively acidic, such as those including a high proportion of citrus juice or vinegar, and do not leave the meat, game, and especially poultry in a marinade too long, otherwise the texture will be adversely affected. Marinades can also be useful in providing a sauce or gravy when cooked with the meat. It is important to use marinade ingredients that have an affinity with the meat, for instance, garlic, rosemary, and red wine for lamb. Dry rubs in the form of ground spices and/or dried herbs, perhaps with the addition of crushed garlic, can be applied all over the surface of the meat, poultry, and game before cooking to enhance the flavor.

LARDING AND BARDING

"Larding" is a technique of adding fat to lean joints of meat or game such as venison that have very little fat on them. It will prevent the joint from drying out during cooking, keeping it moist and tender. Pork fat is normally cut into thin strips or "lardons". Prepare the joint by making incisions in the skin and pushing in the lardons, or by using a sharp knife to make incisions through which strips of fat can be threaded, to cover the whole surface evenly. Another method is to wrap a loin completely in thin strips of lean bacon or pancetta and secure with string.

"Barding" is simply adding fatty bacon to baste the breast of a bird. Barding is particularly important with a big bird such as a turkey but also for many game birds, which have a tendency to dryness. To protect the breast, arrange strips of lean bacon over the breast, which will baste the bird during roasting. Remove the bird 15 minutes before the end of cooking to let the breast brown.

EASY CARVING

To facilitate carving, a joint can be chined, which involves simply loosening the bone in a joint, but leaving it attached. The bone can then be easily cut away before carving. Ask your butcher or meat supplier to chine your joint when buying.

CUTTING AND JOINTING POULTRY AND GAME BIRDS

If you have a whole spring chicken or other small bird that you want to broil or barbecue, you may wish to halve the bird. Simply lay it on its back and cut lengthwise with a sharp knife or poultry shears, cutting down and through the breastbone and then the backbone. To quarter your bird, place the blade of your knife under the leg joint and cut it away from the wing, holding the knife at a 45-degree angle. You will need a sharp, heavy knife for jointing or boning, and poultry shears are also useful.

To joint a chicken and other birds into 8–10 pieces:

1 Put the bird breast upward onto a cutting board. Pull each leg away from the body and slice through the skin and flesh until your knife hits the thigh joint. Push down firmly and twist to break the joint. Cut through the sinews and remaining skin to detach the leg from the body.

2 Cut through the joint to divide the leg into two to give a drumstick and a thigh.

3 Cut each wing off the body.

4 To detach the breast, run a sharp knife along each side of the breastbone and cut away the meat from the carcass, keeping the knife blade against the ribcage as you do so. Either keep the breasts intact or cut each in half, according to your requirements.

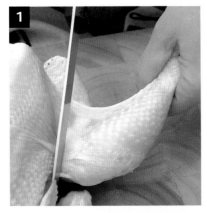

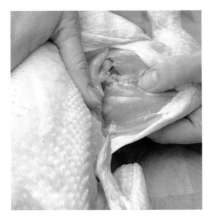

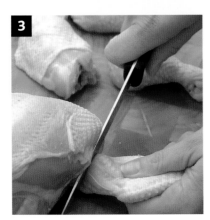

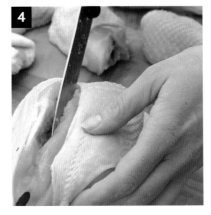

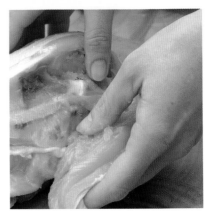

BONING POULTRY AND GAME BIRDS

To bone a chicken, duck, or game bird:

1 Put the bird breast downward onto a cutting board. Cut off the lower wings.

2 Turn the bird over and cut along each side of the breastbone and down, keeping the knife blade against the ribcage, until you reach the wing joint. Cut through the sinews.

3 Hold the wing in one hand and, using the knife, pull the meat away from the bone. Turn the wing inside out and remove the bone.

4 Cut along the side of the bird, freeing the meat, until you reach the leg joint. Cut through the sinews and, using the knife, cut the meat from the bone until you reach the next joint. Cut through the sinews and pull the bone from the flesh. Turn the leg inside out and remove the bone.

5 Cut away the rest of the meat from the ribcage along to the tip of the breastbone and the tail end, then ease out the carcass.

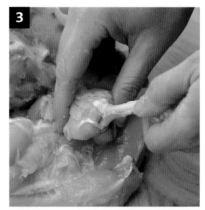

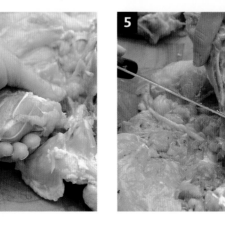

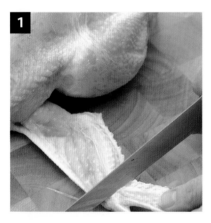

TRUSSING BIRDS

It is important to truss a bird, especially a game bird, to retain its shape during cooking, and also to keep any stuffing in place. The easiest method of trussing is to use a skewer and string.

1 Turn the bird breast downward and fold the neck skin over the back to close the neck opening. Twist the wing tips over the skin to hold it in place.

2 Turn the bird breast upward and, pushing the legs up toward the neck, push a skewer just below the thigh bone right through the body, to emerge just below the thigh on the other side.

3 Turn the bird breast downward again, pull a piece of string across the wing tips, and secure. Loop the string under the ends of the skewer and cross the string again over the center of the back.

4 Turn the bird breast upward again and loop the string around the drumsticks and pope's nose. Pull the string tightly and tie the ends together.

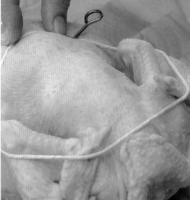

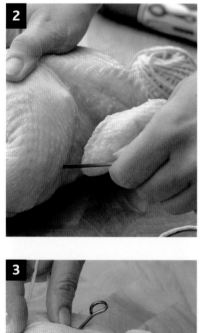

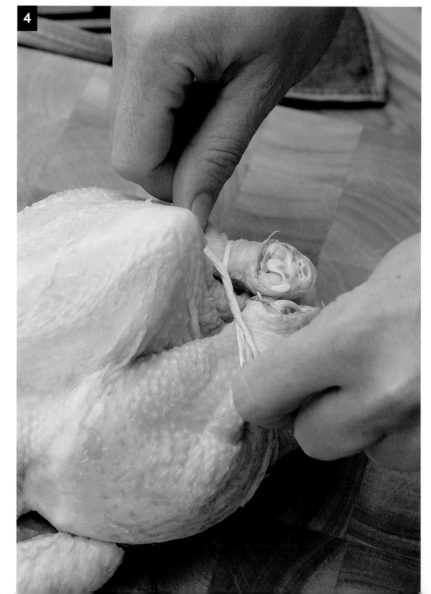

STUFFING

Suitable for both boned and rolled joints of meat, stuffing can provide extra flavor as well as help to keep the roast moist. Hearty stuffings with distinct flavors are needed to complement meat.

In the case of poultry and game, stuffing can be placed either in the neck and cavity of a bird and/or under the breast skin. Stuffing should not fill the whole cavity, or it is unlikely to cook through—the amount of time needed to cook the stuffing will most likely overcook the bird. Stuffing should not go into the bird more than an hour before cooking. Either stuff the opening of the cavity and the neck or loosen the skin between the breast meat and skin and push stuffing under the skin to cover the breast. If you are stuffing a game bird, you might consider partially cooking the stuffing before adding it, so that the bird will remain moist and not overcooked. Alternatively, cook the stuffing separately and simply put a few herbs, butter, or garlic into the bird's cavity.

SPATCHCOCKING POULTRY AND GAME BIRDS

Smaller birds, such as quail and squab chicken, will cook more evenly and quickly when spatchcocked, or flattened, for broiling or barbecuing.

1 Put the bird breast downward onto a cutting board. Cut through the backbone, open the bird out, and press flat.

2 Insert a wooden skewer (presoaked in cold water for 30 minutes) diagonally through the body by pushing it through the thigh and out at the base of the opposite wing.

3 Repeat with a second skewer through the other thigh so that the bird is skewered flat on crossed sticks.

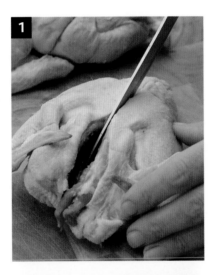

COOKING MEAT, POULTRY, AND GAME

There are no set rules for cooking meat, as each cut requires different preparation, handling, and cooking. However, generally the tender cuts are roasted, broiled, or pan-fried and the tougher cuts require pot-roasting, boiling, braising, or casseroling.

ROASTING TECHNIQUES

Oven roasting is suitable for large joints of meat and whole birds. Quick roasting cooks the meat at a high temperature, which seals the meat and preserves the juices and flavor, but the meat may shrink using this method. Slow roasting cooks the meat at a low temperature over a longer period of time and prevents shrinkage. This method is more likely to produce a tender roast. Check your recipe, as this may advise sealing the meat or bird before roasting or starting the cooking for a short time at a high temperature and then reducing the heat for a longer roasting time. Baste as required during cooking.

ROASTING TIMES

Always weigh a joint or bird to calculate the cooking time. Roasting times vary according to the cut of meat or size and age of the bird, whether on or off the bone and stuffed. The times given below are guidelines only.

Generally, if meat is off the bone it will need slightly longer cooking than a joint on the bone—add ten minutes to the roasting times, and the same for stuffed, rolled joints.

ROASTING RULES

• Always preheat the oven to the correct temperature before putting in the meat or bird.

• Make sure that the joint or bird is at room temperature before roasting.

• When roasting a duck or goose, always use a rack in the roasting pan, so that you can pour off the excess fat.

• If roasting a joint or bird wrapped in foil or in a roasting bag, remember to remove the foil or bag 15 minutes before the end of the cooking time to brown.

• Always rest the meat or bird for the appropriate time, tented with foil, in a warm place.

BEEF

1 Preheat the oven to 450°F/230°C.

2 Roast for 20 minutes, then reduce the temperature to 375°F/190°C and roast for:
• 15 minutes per 1 lb/450 g for rare
• 20 minutes per 1 lb/450 g for medium
• 30 minutes per 1 lb/450 g for well done.

Meat thermometer recommended internal temperature:
Rare: 140°F/60°C
Medium: 160°F/71°C
Well done: 169°F/76°C

LAMB

1 Preheat the oven to 375°F/190°C.

2 Roast for 30 minutes per 1 lb/450 g, 30 minutes less for rare.

Meat thermometer recommended internal temperature: 180°F/82°C

PORK

1 Preheat the oven to 450°F/230°C.

2 Roast for 25 minutes, then reduce the temperature to 375°F/190°C and roast for 35 minutes per 1 lb/450 g.

Meat thermometer recommended internal temperature:
Pork: 189°F/87°C
Bacon or ham joint: 160°F/71°C

TURKEY

1 Preheat the oven to 425°F/220°C.

2 For turkeys weighing 8–10 lb/3.5–4.5 kg, roast for 30 minutes, then reduce the temperature to 325°F/160°C for $2^1/_2$–3 hours, increasing the temperature to 400°F/200°C, uncovered, for the final 30 minutes.

For turkeys weighing 12–14 lb/5.5–6.5 kg, roast for 40 minutes, then reduce the temperature to 325°F/160°C for 3–$3^1/_2$ hours, increasing the temperature to 400°F/200°C, uncovered, for the final 30 minutes.

CHICKEN

1 Preheat the oven to 375°F/190°C.

2 Roast for 20 minutes per 1 lb/450 g, plus 20 minutes. Increase the temperature to 425°F/220°C for the final 15 minutes of the calculated time.

GOOSE

1 Preheat the oven to 425°F/220°C.

2 Roast for 20 minutes, then reduce the temperature to 350°F/180°C and roast for 1 hour 20 minutes to 2 hours.

DUCK

1 Preheat the oven to 425°F/220°C.

2 Roast for 20 minutes, then reduce the temperature to 350°F/180°C and roast for 1 hour– 1 hour 10 minutes.

GAME BIRDS

Woodcock and Snipe
Roast for 15–20 minutes at 450°F/230°C.

Pigeon
Roast for 20 minutes at 425°F/220°C.

Wild Duck
Roast for 20 minutes at 425°F/220°C, then for 10 minutes at 350°F/180°C.

Grouse
Roast for 20 minutes at 425°F/220°C, then for 15 minutes at 350°F/180°C.

Partridge
Roast for 25 minutes at 450°F/230°C.

Pheasant
Roast for 20 minutes at 425°F/220°C, then for 25 minutes at 350°F/180°C.

Guinea Fowl
Roast for 20 minutes at 425°F/220°C, then for 25 minutes at 350°F/180°C.

GRIDDLING OR CHARGRILLING

This is another quick-cooking method suitable for the same cuts as broiling, and offers a convenient indoor alternative to barbecuing. It is also a low-fat method of cooking, as the food can be cooked without any additional oil or fat. For the best results:

• Use a ridged cast-iron grill pan or griddle, which gives the meat attractive charred grilled lines.

• Preheat the grill pan or griddle over high heat until almost smoking, before adding the food and cooking briefly on either side so that it is seared and sealed.

• When cooking duck breasts, score the skin and put skin-side down into the hot pan to release the fat from the skin and keep the flesh moist while making the skin crisp. Turn and cook on the other side after about 8 minutes, depending on the thickness.

BROILING

This quick-cooking method is suitable for small tender cuts such as steaks, chops, and chicken breasts, as well as sausages, burgers, and kabobs. For the best results:

• Always brush the meat or poultry with oil, not the broiler rack.

• Always preheat the broiler before adding the meat.

• Do not wrap the food in foil when broiling, as this will boil it and prevent it from browning and crisping.

• Turn at least once during cooking.

• Do not cook the meat too close to the flame, or it will burn.

BROWNING MEAT

Direct contact between meat and the skillet or broiler burns the surface of the meat, creating irresistible caramelized flavors.

PAN-FRYING

Pan-frying in oil is a quick-cooking method suitable for the same cuts as broiling and griddling or chargrilling. For best results:

• Start cooking over high heat to seal the meat, then reduce the heat and continue to cook until tender.

• Do not overcrowd the pan, as this will boil rather than fry the meat.

DEEP-FRYING

This quick method of cooking is used for meat or poultry with a bread crumb or batter coating, such as chicken drumsticks.
For best results:

• Make sure you have a good depth of oil and heat over high heat to 350–375°F/180–190°C, or until a cube of bread browns in 30 seconds.

• Cook in small batches to prevent the temperature of the oil dropping and the coating becoming soggy.

• Drain the deep-fried food well on paper towels before serving.

BOILING

This cooking method is suitable for joints, mixed meats (as in bollito), salt beef, ham, and bacon joints. Salted joints may need presoaking. The meat can be left to cool in the cooking liquid. For best results:

• Add meat, poultry, or game and vegetables to simmering water.

• Skim regularly to remove any scum that rises to the surface.

• Keep at a regular temperature on a low simmer.

SLOW COOKING

Casseroling and braising, including ragoûts, Carbonnade de Boeuf, and Navarin of Lamb, are all methods of cooking meat slowly in the oven. Stewing, on the other hand, is a slow-cooking method for the stove, with the heat coming from underneath. These long, slow-cooking methods are suitable for tougher cuts of meat, older game birds, chicken, lamb shanks, and chops. Pot-roasting is another long, slow-cooking method using a heavy, lidded pot with a small amount of liquid and vegetables. It is suitable for smaller joints or tougher cuts of meat and older game birds or chicken. Brown the meat or bird, to seal, before pot-roasting.

BARBECUING MEAT, POULTRY, AND GAME

To avoid food poisoning from undercooked or overcooked meat and poultry, follow these rules:

• Keep all marinated meat, poultry, and game in the refrigerator until ready to cook.

• Leave enough time for a charcoal barbecue to reach the right heat—about 45 minutes with ordinary coals. Wait until the coals are glowing red with a powdery gray surface. A gas barbecue needs ten minutes to heat up.

• Do not cook over flames.

• Cook evenly over a steady heat, raising or lowering the grill above the coals, as necessary.

• Cook for a longer time if the temperature is lower.

• Chicken or joints of meat on the bone take a long time to cook, so de-bone before barbecuing.

• Make sure food is piping hot in the center with no red or pink remaining, and with clear juices.

• Be warned that burnt meat can produce harmful chemicals.

• Turn the food regularly to avoid charring or uneven cooking.

• Never partially cook meat or poultry to reheat on a barbecue.

• Never reuse raw meat marinades.

• Keep your barbecue clean.

HOW TO CHECK IF YOUR MEAT/BIRD IS COOKED

It is important to cook meat, poultry, and game properly to make sure that any harmful bacteria have been killed. The following foods should always be cooked until the juices run clear and there is no hint of red or pink remaining:

POULTRY
PHEASANT
PARTRIDGE
PORK
BURGERS
SAUSAGES
KABOBS
ROLLED JOINTS

This rule does not apply to whole cuts of meat (except pork) or joints, which can be cooked rare as long as they have been sealed properly. Steak and chops can also be cooked rare. Bacteria are to be found on the surface of meat, so sealing the meat in a hot skillet or pan will kill any harmful bacteria. Fresh ground meat or ground meat products should be thoroughly cooked through to avoid any risk of food poisoning.

To check if meat, poultry, or game is cooked through, insert a skewer into the thickest part of the meat.

If the juices run clear, it is cooked, but if there is any pinkness or blood, continue cooking for a few minutes and test again.

A meat thermometer is a useful device for checking if a large joint is cooked. It will register the internal temperature of a piece of meat and provide a scale to show when the meat will be cooked. Insert the thermometer into the thickest part of the meat, making sure that it is not touching bone or fat but is well embedded in the flesh.

CARVING POULTRY AND GAME BIRDS

Smaller game birds are often served whole or halved. The same basic technique for carving applies to chicken and most other birds as follows:

• Remove the legs.

• Remove the wings.

• Carve the meat from the breast, slicing downward, with the knife running parallel to the bird.

• Remove any remaining meat from the carcass, including the oysters—the nuggets of flesh either side of the bird on the underside—by hand. The technique of carving the breast

meat can vary to accommodate the size and shape of the bird, as follows:

Duck: Remove the legs and wings and slice the meat from the neck end. Slice close to the breastbone and loosen the breast meat before carving the first slice. Holding the knife at a 45-degree angle, cut the remaining breast meat parallel to the first slice.

Goose: Remove the legs and wings and slice the meat from the neck end. Carve long, thick slices of meat along the length of the breast, holding the knife almost flat against the meat.

Turkey: Remove the wings and legs. Carve the dark meat from the legs, holding the knuckle end of the leg and cutting downward. Carve the breast into thin slices downward from the fattest part of the breast on either side of the breastbone.

NUTRITION

Meat plays an important role in a balanced, healthy diet. Its key nutrients are particularly important for certain groups of people, namely the under-fives, teenagers, women of childbearing age, and the elderly.

Meat is a good source of protein as well as vitamins and minerals such as iron, selenium, zinc, and B vitamins, including vitamin B12, which is not present in plant foods, and vitamin D. A major source of easily absorbed iron, eating meat with vegetables and cereals will also aid absorption of the useful amounts of iron those foods have to offer. Protein is essential for growth and repair of the body, so should constitute 15 percent of our daily calorie intake. Poultry and game birds are lean and therefore an excellent source of high-protein, lowfat meat.

When buying meat, the cut you choose can vary greatly in its fat

content. For instance, a lean pork leg joint for roasting has a quarter less fat than pork belly. However, fat is important for giving flavor to the

meat and is also crucial to its tenderness, so if you want to remove all the visible fat, leave it in place until the meat has been cooked and then trim if necessary. So-called "cheap" cuts of meat can often be the tastiest and most nutritious, so try experimenting with new cuts and methods of cooking.

RECOMMENDED AMOUNTS OF PROTEIN	
MEN	44–55 g per day
WOMEN	42–45 g per day
CHILDREN AGED 4–6	15–20 g per day
CHILDREN AGED 7–10	23–28 g per day

2

PÂTÉS, TERRINES, AND SOUPS

Try these tempting treats for melt-in-the mouth nibbles or first courses. You can create all kinds of pâtés and terrines in a matter of minutes if you've got a food processor—use these recipes to inspire you, and try variations according to your tastes. There is also a selection of hearty soups, from Chicken, Squash, and Spinach Soup to Lamb and Potato Soup, which are substantial enough to serve as meals on their own.

PORK AND PISTACHIO TERRINE

MAKES 15–20 SLICES

Put the pork, veal, pig's liver, pork fat, brandy, garlic, parsley, salt, thyme, allspice, and pepper to taste in a large bowl and use your hands to mix together. Cover and let chill for at least 8 hours and up to 24.

Preheat the oven to 325°F/ 160°C. Lightly grease the base and sides of a 1.5-quart rectangular ceramic terrine. Put the bacon strips on a cutting board and use the back of a knife to stretch gently until almost double in length. Use to line the base and sides of the terrine, laying them next to each other, so that the excess hangs over both long sides.

To check if the seasoning of the meat mixture needs adjusting, heat a small skillet over medium–high heat, add a small amount of the mixture and cook through. Taste and adjust the seasoning, if necessary. Stir the pistachios into the meat mixture.

Spoon one-third of the meat mixture into the terrine, pressing it down well. Lay half the chicken slices on top, pointing from short end to short end, and add a few chives, pointing in the same direction. Repeat this layering, ending with a layer of meat mixture.

Fold over the overhanging strips of bacon to cover the top of the meat mixture. Cover the terrine with the lid and put in a roasting pan. Bring a kettle of water to a boil and pour enough water into the roasting pan to come halfway up the sides of the terrine.

Cook in the preheated oven for 1½ hours, or until the mixture pulls away from the sides of the terrine and the juices run clear. When a metal skewer is inserted into the small hole in the terrine lid, it should come out hot.

Remove the terrine from the water and let it stand for 5 minutes. Uncover the terrine and pour off most of the excess juices, then set aside to cool completely.

Meanwhile, position a loaf pan on top and weigh it down. Let chill for 24–48 hours.

To serve, run a round-bladed knife around the edge of the terrine to loosen, then set the base in a sink of very hot water for 20–30 seconds. Put a serving dish on top of the terrine, then carefully invert both, giving a sharp shake halfway over, and lift off the terrine. Leave to return to room temperature, then use a serrated knife to slice.

12 oz/350 g coarsely ground fresh pork

9 oz/250 g coarsely ground fresh veal

7 oz/200 g pig's liver, finely chopped

7 oz/200 g pork fat, diced

½ cup brandy

2 large garlic cloves, very finely chopped

2 tbsp chopped fresh flat-leaf parsley

1 tsp salt

¾ tsp dried thyme

large pinch of ground allspice

butter, for greasing

10–12 rindless unsmoked lean bacon strips

⅜ cup shelled pistachios, coarsely chopped

2 skinless, boneless chicken breasts, about 6 oz/175 g each, cut into thin strips

small handful of fresh chives, snipped

pepper

CHICKEN AND ASPARAGUS TIMBALES

MAKES 4

1 lemon

2 skinless, boneless chicken breasts, about 4 oz/115 g each

2 fresh tarragon sprigs

²/₃ cup water

4 oz/115 g fresh young asparagus spears, trimmed

2 tbsp dry white wine

¹/₄ oz/10 g powdered gelatin

generous ³/₈ cup cream cheese

1 tsp chopped fresh tarragon

salt and pepper

Pare a strip of rind from the lemon. Squeeze the juice and set aside. Put the lemon rind, chicken, tarragon sprigs, and water in a pan and season to taste with salt and pepper. Cover, bring to a boil, then reduce the heat to low and cook for 20 minutes, or until the meat is tender. Remove the chicken with a slotted spoon and let cool. Strain and set aside the cooking liquid.

Bring a large pan of water to a boil. Add the asparagus and blanch for 5 minutes. Drain, then cut off and set aside 1¹/₂ inches/4 cm of the tips. Chop the stalks.

Put the reserved cooking liquid in a pitcher. Make up to ²/₃ cup with water, if necessary. Stir in the wine. Put 4 tablespoons of the mixture in a heatproof bowl, sprinkle ¹/₂ teaspoon of the gelatin on top and let soak for 2 minutes. Set over a pan of simmering water and stir for 2–3 minutes. Divide between 4 ramekins and let chill for 5 minutes. Arrange 2 asparagus tips, facing in opposite directions, in each ramekin and chill until set. Dissolve the remaining gelatin in the remaining stock and wine in the same way as before.

Chop the chicken, then process in a food processor until smooth. Add the reserved lemon juice, cream cheese, and gelatin mixture and mix briefly. Transfer to a bowl, stir in the asparagus stalks and chopped tarragon, and season to taste with salt and pepper. Divide between the ramekins and let chill for 1 hour, or until set.

To serve, dip the ramekin bases in hot water and invert onto 4 plates.

CHICKEN AND MIXED HERB PÂTÉ

Cook the diced potato in a pan of boiling water for 10 minutes, or until tender, then drain well.

Transfer the potato to a food processor, then add the chicken, garlic, parsley, cilantro, lemon rind and juice, and salt and pepper to taste. Process until thoroughly blended. Alternatively, finely chop all the ingredients and mix together until thoroughly blended.

Put the mixture in a large bowl and stir in the cream cheese. Cover and let chill for 45 minutes.

Remove the pâté from the refrigerator and divide between individual serving dishes. Sprinkle over the sliced scallion to garnish and serve with pita bread triangles, vegetable crudités, and lemon wedges.

SERVES 4

1 small mealy potato, diced

9 oz/250 g cooked skinless chicken, diced

1 garlic clove, crushed

1 tbsp chopped fresh parsley

1 tbsp chopped fresh cilantro

$\frac{1}{2}$ tbsp grated lemon rind

2 tbsp lemon juice

generous $\frac{3}{8}$ cup cream cheese

salt and pepper

sliced scallion, to garnish

TO SERVE

pita bread, cut into triangles

vegetable crudités, such as carrots and celery

lemon wedges

HAM AND PARSLEY TERRINE

MAKES 15–20 SLICES

4 gelatin leaves

1¹/₂ cups dry white wine

generous 1 cup warm water

2 tbsp unsalted butter

2 shallots, very finely chopped

1 garlic clove, crushed

1¹/₂ oz/40 g fresh flat-leaf
parsley, finely chopped

1 piece ham, weighing
10¹/₂ oz/300 g, cut into
¹/₂-inch/1-cm cubes

pepper

Put the gelatin leaves in a bowl with enough cold water to cover and let soak for 5 minutes. Meanwhile, put the wine and water in a pan over medium heat and heat just until small bubbles begin to appear around the edge, without boiling.

Melt the butter in a pan over medium heat. Add the shallots and garlic and cook, stirring frequently, for 3 minutes, or until softened but not browned. Transfer to a heatproof bowl and set aside. Stir the parsley into the bowl and add pepper to taste.

Use your hands to lift the gelatin leaves out of the water and squeeze to remove the excess liquid. Remove the pan with the simmering liquid from the heat, add the gelatin, and stir until dissolved. Add to the parsley mixture.

Rinse the inside of a 1.5-quart rectangular terrine with water, but do not dry. Pour a ¹/₄-inch/5-mm layer of the gelatin mixture into the base of the terrine. Let chill for 30 minutes, or until beginning to set.

Scatter one-third of the ham over the gelatin, pressing it slightly into the gelatin. Let chill for 30 minutes, or until completely set.

Top the ham with one-third of the remaining gelatin, then chill until starting to set. Add another third of the ham and let chill for 30 minutes, or until set. Continue layering and chilling until all the ingredients are used up, ending with a layer of gelatin. Cover the terrine and let chill at least overnight, or for up to 2 days.

To serve, run a round-bladed knife around the edge of the terrine. Put a serving dish on top of the terrine, then carefully invert both, giving a sharp shake halfway over, and lift off the terrine. Cut the terrine into slices and serve.

CHICKEN LIVER PÂTÉ

Transfer the chicken liver mixture to a food processor and process until smooth. Add the remaining butter, cut into small pieces, and process again until creamy.

Press the pâté into a serving dish or 4 small ramekins, smooth the surface, and cover. Store in the refrigerator. If it is to be kept for more than 2 days, you could seal the surface by pouring over a little clarified butter and leaving to set.

Serve the pâté accompanied by brown toast fingers.

SERVES 4

⁵/₈ cup butter

1 onion, finely chopped

1 garlic clove, finely chopped

9 oz/250 g chicken livers

¹/₂ tsp Dijon mustard

2 tbsp brandy (optional)

salt and pepper

brown toast fingers, to serve

Melt half the butter in a large skillet over medium heat. Add the onion and cook, stirring frequently, for 3–4 minutes until softened but not browned. Add the garlic and cook, stirring, for 2 minutes.

Check the chicken livers and remove the cores and any discolored parts using a pair of scissors. Add the livers to the skillet and cook over medium–high heat, stirring frequently, for 5–6 minutes until browned all over.

Season well with salt and pepper and stir in the mustard and brandy, if using.

CONSOMMÉ WITH EGG AND LEMON SAUCE

SERVES 4–6

generous 6¹/₃ cups chicken stock

scant ¹/₃ cup risotto or other short-grain rice

2 eggs

6 tbsp fresh lemon juice

salt and pepper

thin lemon slices, to garnish

Pour the stock into a large pan and bring to a boil. Add the rice and return to a boil, then reduce the heat and simmer for 15–20 minutes, or according to the package directions, until tender.

Meanwhile, put the eggs and lemon juice in a bowl and whisk together until frothy.

When the rice is cooked, reduce the heat and, whisking constantly, gradually add a ladleful of the stock to the lemon mixture. Pour the mixture into the soup and simmer, still whisking, until the soup thickens slightly. (Do not boil the mixture or it will curdle.) Season to taste with salt and pepper.

Ladle the soup into individual serving bowls and garnish each with slices of lemon. Serve hot.

FRAGRANT CHICKEN SOUP

Remove the tough outer leaves from the lemon grass stalks. Using a sharp knife, slice the soft, inner parts diagonally into chunks.

Pour the coconut milk into a large, heavy-bottomed pan and add the lemon grass, lime leaves, and galangal. Bring to a boil, then reduce the heat and simmer for 2 minutes.

Add the water and return to a boil. Add the chicken strips, mushrooms, and tomatoes, reduce the heat, and simmer for 5 minutes, or until the chicken strips are cooked through and tender.

Stir in the chiles, lime juice, and fish sauce. Using a slotted spoon, remove and discard the lemon grass and galangal.

Ladle into 4 large, warmed soup bowls, garnish with a few cilantro leaves, and serve immediately.

SERVES 4

2 lemon grass stalks

1³/₄ cups coconut milk

3 kaffir lime leaves, torn into small pieces

2-inch/5-cm piece galangal or fresh gingerroot, sliced

3 cups water

1 lb 2 oz/500 g skinless, boneless chicken breasts, trimmed of all visible fat and cut into thin strips

8 oz/225 g shiitake mushrooms, chopped

2 tomatoes, cut into wedges

3 fresh Thai chiles, seeded and thinly sliced

3 tbsp lime juice

2 tbsp Thai fish sauce

fresh cilantro leaves, to garnish

BE CAREFUL WHEN HANDLING FRESH CHILES, AS THEY CAN BURN. WEARING RUBBER GLOVES IS A WISE PRECAUTION AND YOU SHOULD ALWAYS WASH YOUR HANDS THOROUGHLY AFTERWARD.

CHICKEN AND PASTA SOUP WITH GUINEA FOWL

Put the chicken and guinea fowl in a large pan with the stock. Bring to a boil and add the onion, peppercorns, cloves, and mace. Reduce the heat and simmer gently for 2 hours, or until the stock is reduced by one third.

Strain the soup and skim off any fat. Return the soup and meat to a clean pan. Add the cream and slowly bring to a boil.

To make a roux, melt the butter in a small pan over low heat. Add the flour and cook, stirring constantly, until it forms a paste-like consistency. Add the roux to the soup and cook, stirring constantly, until slightly thickened.

Just before serving, stir in the cooked spaghetti.

Ladle the soup into individual warmed serving bowls, garnish with the chopped parsley, and serve.

SERVES 6

1 lb 2 oz/500 g skinless, boneless chicken, chopped

1 lb 2 oz/500 g skinless, boneless guinea fowl

2$^{1}/_{2}$ cups chicken stock

1 small onion

6 peppercorns

1 tsp cloves

pinch of mace

$^{2}/_{3}$ cup heavy cream

1 tbsp butter

2 tsp all-purpose flour

4$^{1}/_{2}$ oz/125 g dried spaghetti, broken into short lengths and cooked

2 tbsp chopped fresh parsley, to garnish

CHICKEN, SQUASH, AND SPINACH SOUP

SERVES 4

1 tbsp butter

1 tbsp oil

3 skinless, boneless chicken breasts, about 4 oz/115 g each, cubed

2 small leeks, green parts included, thinly sliced

1 small butternut squash, peeled and cut into $^3/_4$-inch/ 2-cm cubes

1 small fresh green chile (optional), seeded and very finely chopped

14 oz/400 g canned chickpeas, drained and rinsed

$^1/_4$ tsp ground cumin

4 cups chicken stock

$2^1/_2$ cups baby spinach leaves, coarsely chopped

salt and pepper

warm crusty bread, to serve

Melt the butter with the oil in a large pan over medium–low heat. Add the chicken, leeks, squash, and chile, if using. Cover and cook, stirring occasionally, for 10 minutes, until the vegetables are beginning to soften.

Add the chickpeas, cumin, and salt and pepper to taste.

Pour in the stock. Bring to a boil, then reduce the heat and simmer gently for 40 minutes, or until the squash is tender.

Stir in the spinach and cook for an additional 30 seconds, or until the spinach is just wilted.

Serve the soup immediately with warm crusty bread.

DUCK WITH SCALLION SOUP

SERVES 4

2 duck breasts, about 6 oz/
175 g each, skin on

2 tbsp Thai red curry paste

2 tbsp vegetable or
peanut oil

bunch of scallions, chopped

2 garlic cloves, crushed

2-inch/5-cm piece fresh
gingerroot, grated

2 carrots, thinly sliced

1 red bell pepper, seeded and
cut into strips

4 cups chicken stock

2 tbsp sweet chili sauce

3–4 tbsp Thai soy sauce

14 oz/400 g canned straw
mushrooms, drained

Slash the skin of the duck 3 or 4 times with a sharp knife and rub in the curry paste.

Heat a wok or large skillet over high heat. Add the duck breasts, skin-side down, and cook for 2–3 minutes. Turn over, reduce the heat, and cook for an additional 3–4 minutes, or until tender and the juices run clear when a skewer is inserted into the thickest part of the meat. Remove with a slotted spoon and thickly slice. Keep warm.

Heat the oil in the preheated wok or large skillet over high heat. Add half the scallions, the garlic, ginger, carrots, and red bell pepper, and stir-fry for 2–3 minutes. Pour in the stock and add the chili sauce, soy sauce, and mushrooms. Bring to a boil, then reduce the heat and simmer for 4–5 minutes.

Ladle the soup into warmed bowls, top with the duck slices, and garnish with the remaining scallions. Serve immediately.

SPICY BEEF AND NOODLE SOUP

Pour the stock into a large pan and bring to a boil. Meanwhile, heat the oil in a preheated wok or large skillet over high heat. Add one third of the noodles and cook, stirring, for 10–20 seconds, or until puffed up. Lift out with tongs, drain on paper towels, and set aside. Pour off all but 2 tablespoons of the oil.

Add the shallots, garlic, and ginger to the wok and stir-fry for 1 minute. Add the beef and curry paste and stir-fry for 3–4 minutes until tender.

Transfer the beef mixture to the stock with the uncooked noodles, soy sauce, and fish sauce. Simmer for 2–3 minutes until the noodles have swelled.

Serve the soup hot, garnished with chopped cilantro and the reserved crispy noodles.

SERVES 4

4 cups beef stock

²/₃ cup vegetable or peanut oil

3 oz/85 g dried rice vermicelli noodles

2 shallots, thinly sliced

2 garlic cloves, crushed

1-inch/2.5-cm piece fresh gingerroot, thinly sliced

1 steak tenderloin, weighing 8 oz/225 g, cut into thin strips

2 tbsp Thai green curry paste

2 tbsp Thai soy sauce

1 tbsp Thai fish sauce

chopped fresh cilantro, to garnish

GROUND BEEF AND BEAN SOUP

SERVES 4

2 tbsp vegetable oil

1 large onion, finely chopped

2 garlic cloves, finely chopped

1 green bell pepper, seeded and sliced

2 carrots, sliced

14 oz/400 g canned black-eyed peas

1 cup fresh ground beef

1 tsp each ground cumin, chili powder, and paprika

¼ cabbage, sliced

8 oz/225 g tomatoes, peeled and chopped

2½ cups beef stock

salt and pepper

tortilla chips, warmed corn or flour tortillas, to serve

Heat the oil in a large pan over medium heat. Add the onion and garlic and cook, stirring frequently, for 5 minutes, or until softened. Add the green bell pepper and carrots and cook, stirring frequently, for 5 minutes.

Meanwhile, drain the peas, reserving the liquid from the can. Put two-thirds of the peas, reserving the remainder, in a food processor or blender with the pea liquid and process until smooth.

Add the ground beef to the pan and cook, stirring constantly with a wooden spoon to break up the meat, until browned all over. Add the spices and cook, stirring, for 2 minutes. Add the cabbage, tomatoes, stock, and puréed beans and season to taste with salt and pepper. Bring to a boil, then reduce the heat, cover, and simmer for 15 minutes, or until the vegetables are tender.

Stir in the reserved beans, cover, and simmer for 5 minutes.

Ladle the soup into 4 warmed soup bowls and serve with a bowl of tortilla chips or some warmed corn or flour tortillas.

GROUND BEEF AND CILANTRO SOUP

SERVES 4–6

1 cup fresh ground beef

generous 6$^{1}/_{3}$ cups chicken stock

3 egg whites, lightly beaten

1 tsp salt

$^{1}/_{2}$ tsp white pepper

MARINADE

1 tsp salt

1 tsp sugar

1 tsp rice wine or dry sherry

1 tsp light soy sauce

TO SERVE

1 tbsp finely chopped fresh gingerroot

1 tbsp finely chopped scallions

4–5 tbsp finely chopped fresh cilantro, tough stalks discarded

Mix all the ingredients for the marinade together in a bowl. Add the ground beef and turn to coat in the marinade, then cover and let marinate in the refrigerator for 20 minutes.

Pour the stock into a large pan and bring to a boil. Add the marinated ground beef, stirring to break up any clumps, and simmer for 10 minutes.

Slowly add the egg whites, stirring rapidly so that they form fine shreds. Season to taste with salt and pepper.

To serve, divide the ginger, scallions, and cilantro between the bases of individual bowls and pour the soup on top.

LAMB AND POTATO SOUP

SERVES 6

2 eggplants

3 tbsp olive oil

6 lamb shanks

1 small onion, chopped

1³/₄ cups chicken stock

8¹/₂ cups water

14 oz/400 g sweet potato, cut into chunks

2-inch/5-cm piece cinnamon stick

1 tsp ground cumin

2 tbsp chopped fresh cilantro

CHILI SAUCE

2 red bell peppers, roasted, peeled, seeded, and chopped

¹/₂ tsp coriander seeds, dry-fried

1 oz/25 g fresh red chiles, chopped

2 garlic cloves, chopped

2 tsp caraway seeds

olive oil

salt

Preheat the oven to 400°F/200°C. Prick the eggplants all over with a fork, put on a cookie sheet, and bake in the preheated oven for 1 hour. Let cool, then peel and chop.

Heat the oil in a pan over high heat. Add the lamb shanks and cook until browned all over. Add the onion, stock, and water. Bring to a boil, then reduce the heat and simmer for 1 hour.

Meanwhile, to make the chili sauce, put the red bell peppers, coriander seeds, chiles, garlic, and caraway seeds in a food processor and process until well blended. With the motor running, add enough oil through the feed tube to make a paste. Season to taste with salt, then spoon into a jar. Cover with a layer of olive oil, seal, and chill.

Remove the lamb shanks from the stock, cut off the meat, and chop. Add the sweet potato and spices to the stock and bring to a boil. Reduce the heat, cover, and simmer for 20 minutes. Remove the cinnamon stick. Transfer to the food processor and process with the eggplant until smooth. Return to the pan, add the lamb and cilantro, and heat until hot. Serve with the chili sauce.

BACON AND LENTIL SOUP

Heat a large, heavy-bottomed pan or ovenproof casserole over medium heat. Add the bacon and cook, stirring frequently, for 4–5 minutes, or until the fat runs.

Stir in the onion, carrots, celery, turnip, and potato and cook, stirring frequently, for 5 minutes, or until beginning to soften.

Add the lentils and bouquet garni and pour in the water. Bring to a boil, then reduce the heat, cover, and simmer for 1 hour, or until the lentils are tender.

Remove the bouquet garni and season the soup to taste with pepper, and salt if necessary.

Ladle into warmed soup bowls and serve immediately.

SERVES 4

1 lb/450 g rindless thick smoked bacon strips, diced

1 onion, chopped

2 carrots, sliced

2 celery stalks, chopped

1 turnip, chopped

1 large potato, chopped

generous $^3/_8$ cup Puy lentils

1 bouquet garni

4 cups water or chicken stock

salt and pepper

Do not add any salt until the lentils have finished cooking, otherwise they will toughen, which will impair the texture of the soup.

CORN, CHORIZO, AND SMOKED CHILE SOUP

SERVES 6

1 tbsp sunflower-seed or corn oil

2 onions, chopped

1 lb 4 oz/550 g frozen corn kernels, thawed

2¹/₂ cups chicken stock

scant 2 cups milk

4 chipotle chiles, seeded and finely chopped

2 garlic cloves, finely chopped

2 oz/55 g thinly sliced chorizo sausage, casings removed

2 tbsp lime juice

2 tbsp chopped fresh cilantro

salt

Heat the oil in a large, heavy-bottomed pan over low heat. Add the onions and cook, stirring occasionally, for 5 minutes, or until softened. Stir in the corn kernels, cover, and cook for an additional 3 minutes.

Add the stock, half the milk, the chiles and garlic, and season to taste with salt. Bring to a boil, then reduce the heat, cover, and simmer for 15–20 minutes.

Stir in the remaining milk. Set aside about ³/₄ cup of the soup solids, draining off as much liquid as possible. Transfer the remaining soup solids to a food processor or blender and process to a coarse purée.

Return the soup purée to the pan and stir in the reserved soup solids, the chorizo, lime juice, and cilantro.

Reheat the soup to simmering point, stirring constantly.

Ladle the soup into warmed soup bowls and serve immediately.

3

APPETIZERS AND SNACKS

Whether you're cooking for an informal get-together or for a special occasion, these recipes are easy to prepare but impressive in effect. Choose from classic favorites, such as Prunes and Oysters Wrapped in Bacon, Roasted Asparagus with Ham, or Duck Salad, or try out new options, such as Chicken and Spinach Salad with Ginger Dressing, or Cornmeal with Prosciutto. There are also many substantial yet familiar savory snacks with an international twist for you to enjoy, from Broiled Ham or Cheesesteak Sandwiches, to Egg Rolls or Beef Teriyaki Kabobs.

BROILED HAM SANDWICH

Spread half the cheese on 2 slices of bread, then top each with a slice of ham, cut to fit. Sprinkle the ham with all but 2 tablespoons of the remaining cheese, then add the top slices of bread and press down.

To make the white sauce, melt the butter with the oil in a small, heavy-bottomed pan over medium heat. Add the flour and cook, stirring constantly, for 1 minute. Remove from the heat and pour in the milk, stirring constantly. Return to the heat and cook, stirring constantly, for a minute or so until the sauce is smooth and thickened. Remove the sauce from the heat and stir in the remaining cheese and pepper to taste, then set aside and keep warm.

Beat the egg in a soup plate or other flat bowl. Add one sandwich and press down to coat on both sides, then remove from the bowl and repeat with the other sandwich.

Preheat the broiler to high. Line a cookie sheet with foil and set aside. Melt the butter in a sauté pan or skillet over medium–high heat. Add one or both sandwiches, depending on the size of your pan, and cook until golden brown on both sides. Add a little extra butter, if necessary, if you have to cook the sandwiches separately.

Transfer the sandwiches to the foil-lined cookie sheet and spread the white sauce over the top. Cook under the preheated broiler, about 4 inches/10 cm from the heat, for 4 minutes until golden and brown.

SERVES 2

3¹/₂ oz/100 g Gruyère or Emmental cheese, grated

4 slices white bread, crusts trimmed

2 thick slices cooked ham

1 small egg

3 tbsp unsalted butter, plus extra if necessary

WHITE SAUCE

2 tbsp unsalted butter

1 tsp sunflower-seed oil

¹/₂ tbsp all-purpose flour

¹/₂ cup warm milk

pepper

TO VARY THIS SANDWICH TRY ADDING A FRIED EGG TO THE HAM AND CHEESE FILLING. FOR A MORE ROBUST FLAVOR, SPREAD THE BREAD WITH DIJON OR WHOLE GRAIN MUSTARD BEFORE ADDING THE HAM AND CHEESE.

CHEESESTEAK SANDWICHES

SERVES 4

12 oz/350 g boneless rib steak

1 French stick

3 tbsp olive oil

1 onion, thinly sliced

1 green bell pepper, seeded and thinly sliced

2³/₄ oz/75 g provolone or mozzarella cheese, thinly sliced

salt and pepper

hot pepper sauce, to serve

Put the steak in the freezer for about 2 hours before you need it, until partially frozen.

Cut the French stick into 4 equal lengths, then cut each piece horizontally in half. Thinly slice the partially frozen steak across the grain of the meat. Set to one side.

Heat 2 tablespoons of the oil in a large skillet over medium heat. Add the onion and green bell pepper and cook, stirring occasionally, for 10–15 minutes until both vegetables are softened and the onion is golden brown. Push the mixture to one side of the skillet.

Heat the remaining oil in the skillet over medium heat. When hot, add the steak and stir-fry for 4–5 minutes, or until tender. Stir the onion mixture and steak together and season to taste with salt and pepper.

Preheat the broiler to medium. Divide the steak mixture between the 4 bottom halves of bread and top with the cheese. Cook under the preheated broiler for 1–2 minutes until the cheese has melted, then cover with the top halves of bread and press down gently. Serve immediately with hot pepper sauce.

EGG ROLLS

Squeeze out any excess water from the mushrooms and finely slice, discarding any tough stems.

Heat the oil in a preheated wok or deep pan over high heat. Add the pork and stir-fry until browned. Add the soy sauce, bamboo shoots, mushrooms, and salt and stir-fry for 3 minutes.

Add the shrimp and stir-fry for 2 minutes. Add the bean sprouts and stir-fry for 1 minute. Remove from the heat and stir in the scallions. Let cool.

Put a tablespoon of the mixture toward the bottom of an egg roll skin. Roll once to secure the filling, then fold in the sides to create a 4-inch/10-cm piece and continue to roll up. Seal with egg white.

Heat the oil for deep-frying in a wok, deep-fat fryer, or large, heavy-bottomed pan to 350–375°F/180–190°C, or until a cube of bread browns in 30 seconds. Add the rolls, in batches, and cook for 5 minutes, or until golden brown and crisp. Remove with a slotted spoon and drain on paper towels. Keep hot while you cook the remaining rolls.

MAKES 20–25

6 dried shiitake mushrooms, soaked in warm water for 20 minutes

1 tbsp vegetable or peanut oil, plus extra for deep-frying

1 cup fresh ground pork

1 tsp dark soy sauce

3¹/₂ oz/100 g canned bamboo shoots, rinsed, drained, and cut into short thin sticks, or fresh bamboo shoots, boiled in water for 30 minutes, drained, and cut into short thin sticks

pinch of salt

3¹/₂ oz/100 g raw shrimp, shelled, deveined, and chopped

1¹/₂ cups fresh bean sprouts, coarsely chopped

1 tbsp finely chopped scallions

25 egg roll skins

1 egg white, lightly beaten

CRISPY PORK AND PEANUT BASKETS

Preheat the oven to 400°F/200°C. Cut each sheet of phyllo pastry into 24 squares, 2³/₄ inches/7 cm across, to make a total of 48 squares. Brush each square lightly with a little of the oil and arrange the squares in stacks of 4 in 12 small patty pans, pointing outward. Press the pastry down into the patty pans.

Bake the pastry shells in the preheated oven for 6–8 minutes until golden brown.

Meanwhile, heat the remaining oil in a preheated wok over high heat. Add the garlic and stir-fry for 30 seconds. Add the pork and stir-fry for 4–5 minutes until browned.

Add the curry paste and scallions and stir-fry for 1 minute. Stir in the peanut butter, soy sauce, and chopped cilantro. Season to taste with salt and pepper.

Spoon the pork mixture into the phyllo baskets and serve immediately, garnished with cilantro sprigs.

MAKES 12

2 sheets ready-made phyllo pastry, thawed if frozen, each about 16¹/₂ x 11 inches/ 42 x 28 cm

2 tbsp vegetable oil

1 garlic clove, crushed

¹/₂ cup fresh ground pork

1 tsp Thai red curry paste

2 scallions, finely chopped

3 tbsp crunchy peanut butter

1 tbsp light soy sauce

1 tbsp chopped fresh cilantro, plus extra sprigs to garnish

salt and pepper

WHEN USING PHYLLO PASTRY, REMEMBER THAT IT DRIES OUT VERY QUICKLY AND BECOMES BRITTLE AND DIFFICULT TO HANDLE. WORK QUICKLY AND KEEP ANY SHEETS OF PASTRY YOU'RE NOT USING COVERED WITH PLASTIC WRAP AND A DAMP CLOTH.

PRUNES AND OYSTERS WRAPPED IN BACON

Preheat the oven to 400°F/200°C.

Cut 8 bacon strips lengthwise in half. Put on a cutting board and use the back of a knife to stretch gently until almost double in length. Cut each anchovy fillet lengthwise in half. Wrap an anchovy half around each almond and press them into the cavities in the prunes where the pits have been removed. Wrap a bacon strip around each prune and secure with a toothpick.

Cut the remaining 8 bacon strips lengthwise in half. Put on a cutting board and use the back of a knife to stretch gently until almost double in length. Wrap a bacon strip around each oyster and secure with a toothpick.

Put the wrapped prunes and oysters on a cookie sheet and cook in the preheated oven for 10–15 minutes until sizzling hot and the bacon is cooked. Serve hot.

MAKES 32

16 rindless Canadian bacon strips

8 canned anchovy fillets, drained

16 blanched almonds

16 no-soak prunes

16 smoked oysters, drained if canned

CORNMEAL WITH PROSCIUTTO

MAKES 6

2¹/₂ cups water

¹/₂ cup quick-cook cornmeal

¹/₄ cup freshly grated Parmesan cheese

2 tbsp butter, softened

salt and pepper

2 tbsp extra virgin olive oil, plus extra to serve

TOPPING

6 slices prosciutto

3 oz/85 g fontina cheese, cut into 6 slices

12 fresh sage leaves

extra virgin olive oil, for oiling

Line a 6 x 10-inch/15 x 25-cm jelly roll pan with parchment paper and set aside.

Pour the water into a large pan and bring to a boil. Reduce the heat so that it is just simmering and add a large pinch of salt. Add the cornmeal in a steady stream, stirring constantly. Simmer, stirring constantly, for 5 minutes, or until thickened.

Remove from the heat and stir in the Parmesan cheese and butter and season to taste with pepper. Spoon the cornmeal evenly into the prepared pan and smooth the surface with a palette knife. Set aside to cool completely.

Preheat the broiler to high. Oil a cookie sheet and a 3-inch/7.5-cm plain, round pastry cutter. Turn out the cornmeal onto a counter, stamp out 6 circles, and put on the prepared cookie sheet. Brush generously with some of the oil and season to taste with salt and pepper.

Cook under the preheated broiler for 3–4 minutes. Turn the circles over, brush with more of the oil, and cook for an additional 3–4 minutes until golden. Remove from the broiler and, if you are not serving immediately, set the circles aside to cool completely.

Drape a slice of ham on each circle and top with a slice of fontina cheese. Brush the sage leaves with the remaining oil and put 2 on each circle.

Cook the cornmeal circles under the preheated broiler for 3–4 minutes until the cheese has melted and the sage is crisp. Serve immediately, with extra oil for dipping.

CHICKEN STRIPS

Put the chicken breasts between 2 sheets of plastic wrap and beat with the flat end of a meat mallet or with the side of a rolling pin until about ¼ inch/5 mm thick. Slice the chicken diagonally into 1-inch/2.5-cm strips. Put the flour in a plastic bag, add the chicken strips, a few at a time, and shake well to coat each piece.

Heat the oil for deep-frying in a large, heavy-bottomed pan to 350–375°F/180–190°C, or until a cube of bread browns in 30 seconds. Meanwhile, mix together the bread crumbs, coriander, paprika, and salt and pepper to taste and spread out on a plate. Beat the eggs in a soup plate or other flat bowl. Dip the chicken strips in the egg and then in the bread crumb mixture. When the oil is hot, add the strips, in batches, and cook until crisp and golden all over. Remove with a slotted spoon and drain on paper towels. Keep hot while you cook the remaining strips.

Meanwhile, to make the dip, mix the cream cheese, sour cream, and chives together in a serving bowl, season to taste with salt and pepper, and sprinkle with paprika. Transfer the strips to a large serving plate and garnish with lemon wedges. Garnish the dip with chives and serve with the strips.

SERVES 4

4 skinless, boneless chicken breasts, about 4 oz/115 g each

3 tbsp all-purpose flour

sunflower-seed oil, for deep-frying

1½ cups dried bread crumbs

1 tsp ground coriander

2 tsp paprika

2 eggs

salt and pepper

CHEESE AND CHIVE DIP

½ cup cream cheese

⅔ cup sour cream

3 tbsp snipped fresh chives, plus extra whole chives to garnish

paprika, for sprinkling

salt and pepper

lemon wedges, to garnish

WHEN DEEP-FRYING, MAKE SURE THAT THE OIL IS AT THE CORRECT TEMPERATURE BEFORE COOKING. IF IT IS TOO HOT, IT WILL BURN THE FOOD ON THE OUTSIDE, BUT LEAVE THE INSIDE RAW.

CREAMY CHICKEN RAVIOLI

To make the pasta dough, sift the flour and salt onto a clean counter, make a well in the center, and pour in the eggs and oil. Using your fingers, gradually combine the eggs and oil and incorporate the flour. Turn out the dough onto a lightly floured counter and knead until smooth. Halve the dough, wrap each half in plastic wrap, and let rest for 30 minutes before using.

Place the chicken, spinach, prosciutto, and shallot in a food processor and process until blended. Transfer to a bowl, stir in 2 tablespoons of the cheese, the nutmeg, and half the egg. Season with salt and pepper.

Roll out half the pasta dough thinly on a lightly floured counter. Cover with a dish towel and roll out the second piece of dough. Place small mounds of the filling in rows 1½ inches/4 cm apart on one sheet of dough and brush the spaces in between with beaten egg. Place the second piece of dough on top. Press down firmly between the mounds, pushing out any air. Cut into squares, place on a floured dish towel, and let rest for 1 hour.

Bring a large pan of lightly salted water to a boil. Add the ravioli in batches, return to a boil, and cook for 5 minutes. Remove with a slotted spoon and drain on paper towels, then transfer to a warmed dish.

Meanwhile, pour the cream into a skillet, add the garlic, and bring to a boil. Simmer for 1 minute, then add the mushrooms and 2 tablespoons of the remaining cheese. Season and simmer for 3 minutes. Stir in the basil, then pour the sauce over the ravioli. Sprinkle with the remaining cheese, garnish with basil, and serve.

SERVES 4

4 oz/115 g cooked skinless, boneless chicken breast, coarsely chopped

scant ¼ cup cooked spinach leaves

2 oz/55 g prosciutto, coarsely chopped

1 shallot, coarsely chopped

6 tbsp freshly grated romano cheese

pinch of freshly grated nutmeg

2 eggs, lightly beaten

all-purpose flour, for dusting

1¼ cups heavy cream

2 garlic cloves, finely chopped

4 oz/115 g cremini mushrooms, thinly sliced

2 tbsp shredded fresh basil

salt and pepper

fresh basil sprigs, to garnish

PASTA DOUGH

generous 1⅜ cups all-purpose flour, plus extra for dusting

pinch of salt

2 eggs, lightly beaten

1 tbsp olive oil

To cook the chicken breast, put it in a pan with 1 tablespoon lemon juice and just enough water to cover. Season to taste with salt and pepper and poach gently for 10 minutes, or until cooked.

CURRIED CHICKEN

Put the chicken breasts in a large pan with the bay leaf, onion, and carrot. Cover with water and add $^1/_2$ teaspoon salt and the peppercorns. Bring to a boil over a medium heat, then reduce the heat and simmer very gently for 20–25 minutes. Remove from the heat and let the chicken cool in the stock. Set aside $^2/_3$ cup of the stock for the sauce.

Meanwhile, heat the oil in a skillet over low heat. Add the shallots and cook, stirring, for 2–3 minutes until softened but not browned. Stir in the curry paste and cook for an additional 1 minute. Stir in the reserved stock, the tomato paste, and the lemon juice and simmer for 10 minutes until the sauce is quite thick. Let cool. Remove the chicken from the stock, remove and discard the skin, and slice the meat into neat pieces.

Mix the mayonnaise and yogurt together and stir into the sauce. Add the apricots and season to taste with salt and pepper.

Add the chicken to the sauce and stir until well coated. Turn into a serving dish. Cover and let chill for at least 1 hour to allow the flavors to mingle. Serve garnished with the chopped parsley.

SERVES 6

4 skinless, boneless chicken breasts, about 4 oz/115 g each

1 bay leaf

1 small onion, sliced

1 carrot, sliced

4 black peppercorns

1 tbsp olive oil

2 shallots, finely chopped

2 tsp mild curry paste

2 tsp tomato paste

juice of $^1/_2$ lemon

$1^1/_4$ cups mayonnaise

$^2/_3$ cup plain yogurt

$^1/_2$ cup no-soak dried apricots, chopped

salt and pepper

2 tbsp chopped fresh parsley, to garnish

BEEF TERIYAKI KABOBS

Put the steaks in a shallow, nonmetallic dish. To make the sauce, mix the cornstarch and rice wine together in a small bowl, then stir in the remaining sauce ingredients. Pour the sauce over the meat, cover, and let marinate in the refrigerator for at least 2 hours.

Preheat the barbecue. Remove the meat from the sauce and set aside. Pour the sauce into a small pan and bring to a boil. Reduce the heat until it is just simmering, stirring occasionally.

Cut the meat into thin strips and thread, concertina-style, onto several presoaked wooden skewers, alternating each strip of meat with the pieces of yellow bell pepper and scallion. Cook the kabobs over hot coals for 5–8 minutes, or until the steak is cooked through, turning frequently and basting with the sauce once, halfway through cooking time.

Arrange the skewers on serving plates and pour over the remaining sauce. Serve with salad greens.

SERVES 4

1 lb/450 g extra-thin beef steaks

1 yellow bell pepper, seeded and cut into chunks

8 scallions, cut into short lengths

salad greens, to serve

SAUCE

1 tsp cornstarch

2 tbsp rice wine or dry sherry

2 tbsp white wine vinegar

3 tbsp soy sauce

1 tbsp dark brown sugar

1 garlic clove, crushed

$\frac{1}{2}$ tsp ground cinnamon

$\frac{1}{2}$ tsp ground ginger

ROASTED ASPARAGUS WITH HAM

To make the romesco sauce, preheat the oven to 350°F/180°C. Place the tomatoes, almonds, and garlic on a cookie sheet and roast in the preheated oven for 20 minutes, but check the almonds after about 7 minutes, because they can burn quickly; remove as soon as they are golden and giving off an aroma.

Peel the roasted garlic and tomatoes. Put the almonds, garlic, sweet chile, and dried red chiles in a food processor and process until finely chopped. Add the tomatoes and sugar and process again.

With the motor running, slowly add the olive oil through the feed tube. Add 1½ tablespoons of the vinegar and quickly process. Taste and add extra vinegar, if desired, and salt and pepper to taste. Let stand for at least 2 hours.

Meanwhile, increase the oven temperature to 425°F/220°C. Sprinkle a layer of sea salt over the base of a roasting pan that will hold the asparagus spears in a single layer. Brush the asparagus with the oil, then lay the spears in the roasting pan.

Roast in the preheated oven for 12–15 minutes until just tender when pierced with the tip of a knife. Remove from the oven and season to taste with pepper.

As soon as the spears are cool enough to handle, wrap a piece of ham around each.

Arrange the spears wrapped in ham on a serving platter and serve hot, warm, or at room temperature with a small bowl of romesco sauce for dipping. Alternatively, serve on individual plates with a little romesco sauce.

SERVES 4–6

24 fresh young asparagus spears, trimmed

1–2 tbsp extra virgin olive oil

12 thin slices serrano ham, halved lengthwise

sea salt and pepper

ROMESCO SAUCE

4 large, ripe tomatoes

16 blanched almonds

3 large garlic cloves, unpeeled and left whole

1 dried sweet chile, soaked for 20 minutes and patted dry

4 dried red chiles, soaked for 20 minutes and patted dry

pinch of sugar

²⁄₃ cup extra virgin olive oil

about 2 tbsp red wine vinegar

salt and pepper

TURKEY AND RICE SALAD

SERVES 4

4 cups chicken stock

scant 1 cup mixed long-grain and wild rice

2 tbsp sunflower-seed or corn oil

8 oz/225 g skinless, boneless turkey breast, trimmed of all visible fat and cut into thin strips

8 oz/225 g snow peas

4 oz/115 g oyster mushrooms, torn into pieces

generous $^{1}/_{3}$ cup shelled pistachios, finely chopped

2 tbsp chopped fresh cilantro

1 tbsp snipped fresh garlic chives, plus extra whole garlic chives to garnish

1 tbsp balsamic vinegar

salt and pepper

Set aside 3 tablespoons of the stock and pour the remainder into a large pan and bring to a boil. Add the rice and cook for 30 minutes, or until tender. Drain and let cool slightly.

Meanwhile, heat 1 tablespoon of the oil in a preheated wok or large skillet over medium heat. Add the turkey and stir-fry for 3–4 minutes, or until cooked through. Using a slotted spoon, transfer the turkey to a dish. Add the snow peas and mushrooms to the wok and stir-fry for 1 minute. Add the reserved stock and bring to a boil, then reduce the heat, cover, and simmer for 3–4 minutes. Transfer the vegetables to the dish and let cool slightly.

Thoroughly mix the rice, turkey, snow peas, mushrooms, pistachios, cilantro, and snipped garlic chives together, then season to taste with salt and pepper. Drizzle with the remaining oil and the vinegar and garnish with whole garlic chives. Serve warm.

BEFORE ADDING ANY OF THE INGREDIENTS TO THE PREHEATED WOK, SWIRL THE OIL GENTLY AND CAREFULLY SO THAT IT COATS THE SIDE AS WELL AS THE BOTTOM OF THE WOK.

CHICKEN AND SPINACH SALAD WITH GINGER DRESSING

SERVES 4

$5^5/8$ cups baby spinach leaves

3 celery stalks, thinly sliced

$^1/_2$ cucumber

2 scallions

3 tbsp chopped fresh parsley

12 oz/350 g boneless roast chicken, thinly sliced

smoked almonds, to garnish (optional)

DRESSING

1-inch/2.5-cm piece fresh gingerroot, finely grated

3 tbsp olive oil

1 tbsp white wine vinegar

1 tbsp honey

$^1/_2$ tsp ground cinnamon

salt and pepper, to taste

Thoroughly wash the spinach leaves, then pat dry with paper towels.

Using a sharp knife, thinly slice the celery, cucumber, and scallions. Toss in a large bowl with the spinach leaves and parsley.

Transfer to serving plates and arrange the chicken on top of the salad.

Put all the ingredients for the dressing into a screw-top jar, screw the lid on tightly, and shake well to mix. Pour over the salad.

Garnish the salad with a few smoked almonds, if you like, and serve immediately.

MIXED GREENS WITH WARM CHICKEN LIVERS

Toss the salad greens with the parsley and chives and divide between individual plates.

Heat 2 tablespoons of the oil in a sauté pan or skillet over medium–high heat. Add the shallots and garlic and cook, stirring, for 2 minutes, or until the shallots are softened but not browned.

Add another tablespoon of the oil to the pan and heat. Add the chicken livers and cook, stirring frequently, for 5 minutes, or until just pink in the center when you cut a piece in half. Add a little extra oil to the pan while the chicken livers are cooking, if necessary.

Increase the heat to high, add the vinegar and quickly stir around. Season to taste with salt and pepper, then spoon the chicken livers and their cooking juices over the mixed greens. Serve immediately with French bread.

SERVES 6–8

9 oz/250 g mixed salad greens, large ones torn into bite-size pieces

2 tbsp chopped fresh flat-leaf parsley

2 tbsp snipped fresh chives

3–4 tbsp olive oil

3^1/$_2$ oz/100 g shallots, finely chopped

1 large garlic clove, finely chopped

1 lb 2 oz/500 g chicken livers, cored, trimmed and halved

3 tbsp raspberry vinegar

salt and pepper

French bread, to serve

DUCK SALAD

SERVES 4

4 boneless duck breasts, about 6 oz/175 g each, skin on

1 lemon grass stalk, broken into 3 and each piece cut in half lengthwise

3 tbsp vegetable or peanut oil

2 tbsp sesame oil

1 tsp Thai fish sauce

1 fresh green chile, seeded and chopped

2 tbsp Thai red curry paste

1/2 fresh pineapple, peeled and sliced

3-inch/7.5-cm piece cucumber, peeled, seeded, and sliced

3 tomatoes, cut into wedges

1 onion, thinly sliced

DRESSING

juice of 1 lemon

2 garlic cloves, crushed

1 tsp jaggery or light brown sugar

2 tbsp vegetable or peanut oil

Unwrap the duck breasts and let the skin dry out overnight in the refrigerator.

The following day, slash the skin side 5 or 6 times with a sharp knife. Mix the lemon grass, 2 tablespoons of the vegetable oil, the sesame oil, fish sauce, chile, and curry paste together in a shallow dish and add the duck breasts. Turn to coat in the marinade and rub into the meat. Cover and let marinate in the refrigerator for 2–3 hours.

Heat the remaining oil in a preheated wok or large skillet over medium heat. Add the duck, skin-side down, and cook for 3–4 minutes until the skin is browned and crisp and the meat cooked most of the way through.

Turn the breasts over and cook until browned and the meat is cooked to your liking.

Meanwhile, arrange the pineapple, cucumber, tomatoes, and onion on a platter. Whisk all the ingredients for the dressing together in a small bowl and pour over the top.

Remove the duck from the wok with a slotted spoon and thickly slice. Arrange on top of the salad and serve while still hot.

STEAK AND APPLE SALAD

SERVES 4

2 steak tenderloins, about
6 oz/175 g each and 1 inch/
2.5 cm thick

olive or sunflower-seed oil,
for brushing

1 tbsp wholegrain mustard

$^2/_3$ cup mayonnaise

1 tbsp lemon juice

1 lb 2 oz/500 g eating apples

4 celery stalks, thinly sliced

$^5/_8$ cup walnut halves,
broken into pieces

$3^1/_2$ oz/100 g mixed
salad greens

pepper

Heat a thick, cast-iron grill pan or heavy-bottomed skillet over medium heat. Brush each steak with oil and season to taste with pepper. When hot, add the steaks to the pan and cook for 6–7 minutes for rare or 8–10 minutes for medium, turning the steaks frequently and brushing once or twice with oil. Remove from the pan and set aside.

Meanwhile, stir the mustard into the mayonnaise. Put the lemon juice into a large bowl. Peel and core the apples, then cut into small chunks and immediately toss in the lemon juice to prevent discoloration. Stir in the mustard mayonnaise. Add the celery and walnuts and toss together.

Arrange the salad greens on 4 plates, then divide the apple mixture between them. Very thinly slice the steaks, arrange on top of the salad, and serve immediately.

PEPPERED BEEF SALAD

Rinse the steaks and pat dry with paper towels. Mix the peppercorns with the five-spice powder and press onto both sides of the steaks.

Heat a ridged grill pan over high heat or preheat a broiler to high. Cook the steaks in the hot pan or under the preheated broiler for 2–3 minutes each side, or until cooked to your liking.

Meanwhile, mix the bean sprouts, half the ginger, the shallots, and red bell pepper together in a bowl and divide between 4 plates. Mix the remaining ginger, soy sauce, chiles, lemon grass, and oils together in a separate small bowl.

Slice the beef and arrange on top of the vegetables. Drizzle with the dressing and serve immediately.

SERVES 4

4 steak tenderloins, about 4 oz/115 g each

2 tbsp black peppercorns, crushed

1 tsp Chinese five-spice powder

$^3/_4$ cup fresh bean sprouts

1-inch/2.5-cm piece fresh gingerroot, finely chopped

4 shallots, thinly sliced

1 red bell pepper, seeded and thinly sliced

3 tbsp Thai soy sauce

2 fresh red chiles, seeded and sliced

$^1/_2$ lemon grass stalk, finely chopped

3 tbsp vegetable or peanut oil

1 tbsp sesame oil

ARTICHOKE AND PROSCIUTTO SALAD

Make sure that the artichoke hearts are thoroughly drained, then cut into quarters and put in a bowl. Cut each fresh tomato into wedges. Slice the sun-dried tomatoes into thin strips. Cut the prosciutto into thin strips and add to the bowl with the tomatoes and olive halves.

Setting aside a few whole basil leaves for garnishing, tear the remainder into small pieces and add to the bowl containing the other salad ingredients.

Put all the ingredients for the dressing into a screw-top jar, screw the lid on tightly, and shake well to mix.

Pour the dressing over the salad and toss together. Serve the salad immediately, garnished with the reserved basil leaves.

SERVES 4

9$\frac{1}{2}$ oz/275 g canned artichoke hearts in oil, drained

4 small tomatoes

$\frac{1}{8}$ cup sun-dried tomatoes in oil, drained

1$\frac{1}{2}$ oz/40 g prosciutto

scant $\frac{1}{4}$ cup pitted black olives, halved

handful of fresh basil leaves

DRESSING

3 tbsp olive oil

1 tbsp white wine vinegar

1 garlic clove, crushed

$\frac{1}{2}$ tsp mild mustard

1 tsp honey

salt and pepper

USE BOTTLED ARTICHOKES IN OIL IF YOU CAN FIND THEM BECAUSE THEY HAVE A BETTER FLAVOR.

4

MAIN COURSES

Meat takes pride of place in this selection of classic dishes that are drawn from traditional cuisine around the world. You'll find plenty of ideas for everyday meals for friends and family and simple yet sophisticated dishes for when you want to entertain in style. If you're in the mood for Chicken with Saffron Mash or just a simple Broiled Steak, you'll find the recipe here. Venture further afield with Lamb Meatballs, Aromatic Duck, or Lentils with Sausage, or try out some Chicken Fajitas.

CHICKEN WITH SAFFRON MASH

Put the potatoes, garlic, and saffron in a large, heavy-bottomed pan, add the stock, and bring to a boil. Reduce the heat, cover, and simmer for 20 minutes, or until tender.

Meanwhile, brush the chicken breasts all over with half the oil and the lemon juice. Sprinkle with the chopped thyme, fresh cilantro, and crushed coriander seeds. Heat a grill pan over medium–high heat, add the chicken, and cook for 5 minutes on each side, or until the juices run clear when a skewer is inserted into the thickest part of the meat. Alternatively, cook the chicken breasts under a preheated hot broiler for 5 minutes on each side, or until cooked through.

Drain the potatoes and return the contents of the strainer to the pan. Add the remaining oil and the milk, season to taste with salt and pepper, and mash until smooth.

Divide the saffron mash between 4 large, warmed serving plates, top with a cooked chicken breast, and garnish with a few thyme sprigs. Serve immediately.

SERVES 4

1 lb 4 oz/550 g mealy potatoes, cut into chunks

1 garlic clove, peeled and sliced

1 tsp saffron threads, crushed

5 cups chicken or vegetable stock

4 skinless, boneless chicken breasts, about 4 oz/115 g each, trimmed of all visible fat

2 tbsp olive oil

1 tbsp lemon juice

1 tbsp chopped fresh thyme, plus extra sprigs to garnish

1 tbsp chopped fresh cilantro

1 tbsp coriander seeds, crushed

generous $1/3$ cup hot lowfat milk

salt and pepper

CHICKEN FAJITAS

Put all the ingredients for the marinade in a large, shallow, nonmetallic dish or bowl and mix together well.

Slice the chicken across the grain into slices 1 inch/2.5 cm thick. Toss in the marinade until well coated. Cover and let marinate in the refrigerator for 2–3 hours, turning occasionally.

Heat a grill pan over medium–high heat. Remove the chicken slices from the marinade with a slotted spoon, add to the grill pan, and cook for 3–4 minutes on each side until cooked through. Transfer to a warmed serving plate and keep warm.

Add the red bell peppers, skin-side down, to the grill pan and cook for 2 minutes on each side. Transfer to the serving plate.

Pile the cooked chicken and bell peppers onto the warmed tortillas, along with some guacamole, sour cream, tomato salsa, and shredded lettuce. Serve with refried beans or boiled rice, if you like.

SERVES 4

4 skinless, boneless chicken breasts, about 4 oz/115 g each

2 red bell peppers, seeded and cut into 1-inch/2.5-cm strips

8 flour tortillas, warmed

ready-made guacamole

sour cream

tomato salsa

shredded iceberg lettuce

refried beans or boiled rice, to serve (optional)

MARINADE

3 tbsp olive oil, plus extra for drizzling

3 tbsp maple syrup or honey

1 tbsp red wine vinegar

2 garlic cloves, crushed

2 tsp dried oregano

1–2 tsp crushed dried red chiles

salt and pepper

BROILED CHICKEN WITH LEMON

Prick the skin of the chicken quarters all over with a fork. Put the chicken in a nonmetallic dish, add the lemon juice, oil, garlic, thyme, and salt and pepper to taste and mix together well. Cover and let marinate in the refrigerator for at least 2 hours.

To cook the chicken, preheat the broiler to medium. Put the chicken in the broiler pan and baste with the marinade. Cook under the preheated broiler, turning occasionally and basting with the marinade, but not for the last 10 minutes of the cooking time, for 30–40 minutes until the chicken is tender and the juices run clear when a skewer is inserted into the thickest part of the meat.

Serve hot, garnished with the lemon rind and a few thyme sprigs.

SERVES 4

4 chicken quarters

juice and grated rind of 2 lemons

4 tbsp olive oil

2 garlic cloves, crushed

2 fresh thyme sprigs, plus extra to garnish

salt and pepper

SERVES 6–8

2 pinches of saffron threads

4 tablespoons hot water

scant 2 cups Spanish short-grain rice

16 live mussels

about 6 tbsp olive oil

6–8 unboned chicken thighs, skin on, excess fat removed

5 oz/140 g chorizo sausage, casing removed, cut into 1/4-inch/5-mm slices

2 large onions, chopped

4 large garlic cloves, crushed

1 tsp mild or hot Spanish paprika, to taste

3 1/2 oz/100 g green beans, chopped

scant 1 cup frozen peas

5 cups fish, chicken, or vegetable stock

16 raw shrimp, shelled and deveined

2 red bell peppers, broiled, peeled, seeded, and sliced

1 1/4 oz/35 g fresh parsley, finely chopped

salt and pepper

PAELLA WITH CHICKEN AND CHORIZO

Put the saffron threads and water in a small bowl and let soak. Put the rice in a strainer and rinse in cold water until the water runs clear. Set aside. Clean the mussels by scrubbing or scraping the shells and pulling out any beards that are attached to them. Discard any with broken shells or any that refuse to close when tapped. Set aside.

Heat 3 tablespoons of the oil in a 12-inch/30-cm paella pan or ovenproof casserole over medium–high heat. Add the chicken, skin-side down, and cook for 5 minutes, or until golden and crisp. Transfer to a bowl. Add the chorizo and cook for 1 minute, or until it starts to crisp. Add to the chicken.

Heat another 3 tablespoons of oil in the paella pan. Add the onions and cook, stirring, for 2 minutes, then add the garlic and paprika and cook, stirring, for an additional 3 minutes until the onions are softened but not browned.

Add the drained rice, beans, and peas and stir until coated in oil. Return the chicken thighs and chorizo and any accumulated juices

to the pan. Stir in the stock, saffron and its soaking liquid, and salt and pepper to taste. Bring to a boil, stirring constantly.

Reduce the heat to low and simmer, without stirring, for 15 minutes, or until the rice is almost tender and most of the liquid is absorbed.

Arrange the mussels, shrimp, and bell pepper strips on top, cover the pan, and simmer, without stirring, for an additional 5 minutes, or until the shrimp become pink and the mussels are opened.

Discard any mussels that remain closed. Taste and adjust the seasoning. Sprinkle with the parsley and serve immediately.

THE FIRST TIME YOU MAKE THIS, PREHEAT THE OVEN TO 375°F/190°C WHILE THE PAELLA SIMMERS. HEAT SOURCES ARE NOT CONSISTENT ON STOVES, SO IT IS HARD TO SAY HOW LONG IT TAKES FOR THE LIQUID TO BE ABSORBED. IF THERE IS TOO MUCH LIQUID ON THE SURFACE, PUT THE DISH IN THE OVEN, COVER, AND BAKE FOR 10 MINUTES, OR UNTIL VERY LITTLE LIQUID REMAINS.

CHICKEN WITH VEGETABLES AND CILANTRO RICE

Heat the oil in a preheated wok or large skillet over high heat. Add the onion, garlic, and ginger and stir-fry for 1–2 minutes.

Add the chicken and mushrooms and stir-fry until the chicken is browned. Add the coconut milk, sugar snap peas, soy sauce, and fish sauce and bring to a boil. Reduce the heat and simmer gently for 4–5 minutes until the chicken and vegetables are tender.

To prepare the cilantro rice, heat the oil in a separate preheated wok or large skillet over medium heat. Add the onion and stir-fry until softened but not browned. Add the cooked rice, bok choy, and cilantro and cook, stirring, until the leaves are wilted and the rice is thoroughly hot. Sprinkle over the soy sauce and serve immediately with the chicken.

SERVES 4

2 tbsp vegetable or peanut oil

1 red onion, chopped

2 garlic cloves, chopped

1-inch/2.5-cm piece fresh gingerroot, chopped

2 skinless, boneless chicken breasts, about 4 oz/115 g each, cut into strips

4 oz/115 g white mushrooms

1³/₄ cups canned coconut milk

2 oz/55 g sugar snap peas, halved lengthwise

2 tbsp soy sauce

1 tbsp Thai fish sauce

RICE

1 tbsp vegetable or peanut oil

1 red onion, sliced

1³/₄ cups rice, cooked and cooled

8 oz/250 g bok choy, torn into large pieces

handful of fresh cilantro, chopped

2 tbsp Thai soy sauce

PAPRIKA CHICKEN ON A BED OF ONIONS AND HAM

ovenproof casserole over medium–high heat. Add the chicken breasts, skin-side down, and cook for 5 minutes, or until the skins are crisp and golden. Remove from the skillet.

Stir the ham into the fat remaining in the skillet, cover, and cook for 2 minutes, or until the fat runs. Add the onions and cook, stirring occasionally and adding a little extra oil if necessary, for 5 minutes, or until the onions are softened but not browned.

Add the wine and stock and bring to a boil, stirring. Return the chicken breasts to the skillet and season to taste with salt and pepper. Reduce the heat, cover, and simmer for 20 minutes, or until the chicken is tender and the juices run clear when a skewer is inserted into the thickest part of the meat.

Transfer the chicken to a plate and keep warm in a low oven. Bring the sauce to a boil and cook until the juices have reduced. Taste and adjust the seasoning.

Divide the sauce between 4 individual warmed plates and arrange a chicken breast on top of each. Garnish with thyme sprigs and serve immediately.

Put the chicken in a nonmetallic bowl. Pour over the lemon juice, cover, and let marinate in the refrigerator overnight.

Remove the chicken from the marinade and dry with paper towels. Rub the skins with the paprika and salt and pepper to taste.

Heat 2 tablespoons oil in a large, heavy-bottomed skillet with a lid or

SERVES 4

4 chicken breast fillets, about 4 oz/115 g each, skin on

$2/3$ cup freshly squeezed lemon juice

1–1$1/2$ tsp mild or hot Spanish paprika, to taste

about 2 tbsp olive oil

2$1/2$ oz/70 g serrano ham, diced

4 large onions, thinly sliced

$1/2$ cup dry white wine

$1/2$ cup chicken stock

salt and pepper

fresh thyme sprigs, to garnish

AROMATIC DUCK

SERVES 6–8

1 duckling, weighing 4 lb 8 oz/ 2 kg

1 tsp salt

8 slices fresh gingerroot

3 scallions

3 cloves

1 cinnamon stick

3 tbsp rice wine or dry sherry

1 tsp sesame oil

1 tbsp light soy sauce

2 tsp dark soy sauce

scant $^{1}/_{4}$ cup rock sugar

generous 1 cup water

Rinse the duckling and pat dry with paper towels. Rub the skin with the salt and let stand for 15 minutes. Rinse well.

Stuff the duckling with the ginger and scallions, then put in an ovenproof casserole with all the remaining ingredients. Bring to a boil, then reduce the heat, cover, and simmer for 1 hour.

Remove the duckling from the casserole and cut into chunks.

Transfer the duck pieces to a serving dish. Strain the gravy, skimming off any fat, and pour it over the duck. Serve immediately.

Rock sugar typically comes in the form of transparent blocks that are available from Chinese food stores.

SERVES 4

4 boneless duck breasts, about
6 oz/175 g each, skin on

1 tbsp sunflower-seed oil

$^1/_2$ cup dry white wine

$4^1/_2$ oz/125 g frozen mixed
berries, straight from
the freezer, or fresh berries

1 tbsp honey

$^1/_4$ tsp ground allspice

salt and pepper

DUCK BREASTS
WITH FRUIT SAUCE

Preheat the oven to 400°F/200°C. Finely score each duck breast in a criss-cross pattern through the skin into the fat.

Heat the oil in a large sauté pan or skillet over high heat. Add the duck breasts, skin-side down, and cook for 4 minutes, or until the skin is crisp and golden brown. Using a slotted spoon, transfer the duck breasts to a roasting pan, skin-side up, and roast in the preheated oven for 12 minutes for medium-rare or 15 minutes for medium.

Meanwhile, tip the excess fat out of the sauté pan. Put the pan over high heat, add the wine, and bring to a boil, scraping any sediment from the bottom of the pan. Stir in the fruit, reduce the heat to medium, and let simmer for 5 minutes, or until tender, stirring occasionally and pressing down with the back of a wooden spoon.

Add the honey and allspice and stir until the honey dissolves. Season to taste with salt and pepper and add extra honey or spice, as desired. Reduce the heat to low and let the sauce simmer and reduce, stirring occasionally.

Transfer the duck breasts to a carving board, cover loosely with foil, and let rest for a few minutes. Thinly slice the duck breasts on the diagonal and transfer to warmed serving plates. Add any accumulated duck juices to the sauce and adjust the seasoning, if necessary.

At this point, the sauce can be used as it is, containing pieces of fruit, or processed in a food processor or blender and passed through a nonmetallic strainer to make a smooth sauce, reheating if necessary.

Spoon the fruit sauce over the duck breasts and serve immediately.

VEAL WITH PROSCIUTTO AND SAGE

Put the veal scallops between 2 sheets of plastic wrap and pound with the flat end of a meat mallet or with the side of a rolling pin until very thin. Transfer to a plate and sprinkle with the lemon juice. Cover and let marinate in the refrigerator for 30 minutes, spooning the lemon juice over occasionally.

Pat the scallops dry with paper towels, season to taste with salt and pepper, and rub with half the sage. Put a slice of ham on each scallop. Secure with a toothpick.

Melt the butter in a large, heavy-bottomed skillet over low heat. Add the remaining sage and cook, stirring constantly, for 1 minute. Add the scallops and cook for 3–4 minutes on each side until golden brown. Pour in the wine and cook for an additional 2 minutes.

Transfer the scallops to a warmed serving dish and pour over the pan juices. Remove and discard the toothpicks and serve the scallops immediately.

SERVES 4

4 veal scallops

2 tbsp lemon juice

1 tbsp chopped fresh sage leaves

4 slices prosciutto

4 tbsp unsalted butter

3 tbsp dry white wine

salt and pepper

YOU CAN ALSO PREPARE SKINNED, BONED CHICKEN BREASTS IN THE SAME WAY. IF THEY ARE VERY THICK, CUT THEM IN HALF HORIZONTALLY FIRST.

BRAISED VEAL IN RED WINE

Preheat the oven to 350°F/180°C. Put the flour and pepper to taste in a plastic bag, add the meat, and shake well to coat each piece. Heat the oil in a large, ovenproof casserole. Add the meat, in batches, and cook for 5–10 minutes, stirring constantly, until browned all over. Remove with a slotted spoon and set aside.

Add the whole onions, garlic, and carrots to the casserole and cook, stirring frequently, for 5 minutes until beginning to soften.

Return the meat to the casserole. Pour in the wine, scraping any sediment from the bottom of the casserole, then add the stock, tomatoes with their juice, lemon rind, bay leaf, parsley, basil, thyme, and salt and pepper to taste. Bring to a boil, then cover the casserole.

Transfer to the preheated oven and cook for 2 hours, or until the meat is tender.

Serve hot, garnished with extra chopped parsley and accompanied by boiled rice.

SERVES 6

scant $^1/_4$ cup all-purpose flour

2 lb/900 g stewing veal or beef, cubed

4 tbsp olive oil

12 oz/350 g white onions

2 garlic cloves, finely chopped

12 oz/350 g carrots, sliced

$1^1/_4$ cups full-bodied red wine

$^2/_3$ cup beef or chicken stock

14 oz/400 g canned chopped tomatoes with herbs in juice

pared rind of 1 lemon

1 bay leaf

1 tbsp chopped fresh flat-leaf parsley, plus extra to garnish

1 tbsp chopped fresh basil

1 tsp chopped fresh thyme

salt and pepper

boiled rice, to serve

BROILED STEAK

To make the Maître d'Hôtel butter, put the butter in a bowl and beat with a wooden spoon until softened. Add the parsley and lemon juice, season to taste with salt and pepper, and beat together until thoroughly combined.

Turn out onto a sheet of waxed paper and shape into a roll. Wrap in the waxed paper and let chill for 2–3 hours until firm. Just before serving, slice the butter into thin circles.

Preheat the broiler or barbecue. Brush each steak with oil and season to taste with pepper.

Put the steaks onto an oiled broiler rack and cook under or over medium heat for the required length of time and according to your taste: for $^3/_4$-inch/2-cm thick steaks, 5 minutes for rare, 8–10 minutes for medium, and 12–14 minutes for well done; for 1-inch/2.5-cm thick steaks, 6–7 minutes for rare, 8–10 minutes for medium, and 12–15 minutes for well done; for $1^1/_2$-inch/4-cm thick steaks, 10 minutes for rare, 12–14 minutes for medium, and 18–20 minutes for well done. During cooking, turn the steaks frequently, using a spatula rather than a sharp tool so that you don't pierce the meat and allow the juices to escape. When you turn the steaks, brush them once or twice with oil. Watch the steaks constantly during cooking to ensure that they don't overcook.

Serve immediately, with each steak topped with a slice of Maître d'Hôtel butter and accompanied by a baked potato and green salad.

SERVES 6

6 rump, sirloin or steak tenderloins, about 6–8 oz/ 175–225 g each

olive or sunflower-seed oil, for brushing and oiling

pepper

MAITRE D'HOTEL BUTTER

8 tbsp butter

3 tbsp finely chopped fresh parsley

1 tbsp lemon juice

salt and pepper

TO SERVE

baked potatoes

green salad

IF THE STEAKS HAVE A PIECE OF FAT RUNNING ALONG THEM, CUT OR SNIP INTO IT AT REGULAR INTERVALS TO PREVENT THE STEAKS FROM CURLING DURING COOKING. A BAKED POTATO AND SALAD HAS BEEN SUGGESTED AS HEALTHY ACCOMPANIMENTS, BUT YOU COULD SERVE THE STEAKS WITH FRENCH FRIES AND BATTERED DEEP-FRIED ONION RINGS INSTEAD.

PEPPERED T-BONE STEAKS

SERVES 2

2 tbsp black peppercorns, green peppercorns or a mixture of both

2 T-bone steaks, about 9 oz/ 250 g each

2 tbsp butter

1 tbsp olive or sunflower-seed oil

$^1/_2$ cup red wine

salt

TO SERVE

green beans

long-grain rice, cooked with turmeric for added color

Put the peppercorns in a mortar and crush coarsely with a pestle. Alternatively, put in a strong plastic bag, put on a cutting board, and crush coarsely with the end of a rolling pin.

Spread the crushed peppercorns (removing the 'dust') out on a plate and press one side of each steak hard into them to encrust the surface of the meat. Turn the steak over and repeat with the other side.

Melt the butter with the oil in a large, heavy-bottomed skillet over high heat. When hot, add the steaks and cook quickly on both sides to

seal. Reduce the heat to medium and cook, turning once, for $2^1/_2$–3 minutes each side for rare, $3^1/_2$–5 minutes each side for medium, or 5–7 minutes each side for well done. Transfer the steaks to warmed plates and keep warm.

Add the wine to the skillet and stir, scraping any sediment from the bottom of the skillet. Bring to a boil and continue to boil until reduced by about half. Season to taste with salt.

Pour the pan juices over the steaks and serve immediately with green beans and rice.

BAKED PASTA WITH SPICY MEAT SAUCE

Preheat the oven to 375°F/190°C. Heat the oil in a pan over medium heat. Add the onion and garlic and cook, stirring frequently, for 5 minutes, or until the onion is softened. Add the ground meat and cook, stirring constantly with a wooden spoon to break up the meat, for 5 minutes, or until browned all over.

Add the tomatoes with their juice, sugar, herbs, spices, and salt and pepper to taste. Bring to a boil, then reduce the heat and let simmer, uncovered, for 30 minutes, stirring occasionally.

Meanwhile, cook the pasta in a large pan of boiling salted water for 10–12 minutes, or according to the package directions, until tender but still firm to the bite. Drain well. Beat the eggs, yogurt, feta cheese, and salt and pepper to taste together in a bowl.

Transfer the meat mixture to a large ovenproof dish. Add the pasta in a layer to cover the meat, then pour over the yogurt mixture. Sprinkle over the romano cheese.

Bake in the preheated oven for 30–45 minutes until golden brown. Serve hot or warm.

SERVES 4–6

2 tbsp olive oil

1 onion, finely chopped

2 garlic cloves, finely chopped

1 lb 7 oz/650 g lean fresh ground lamb or beef

14 oz/400 g canned chopped tomatoes in juice

pinch of sugar

2 tbsp chopped fresh flat-leaf parsley

1 tbsp chopped fresh marjoram

1 tsp ground cinnamon

1/2 tsp freshly grated nutmeg

1/4 tsp ground cloves

8 oz/225 g dried macaroni or other short pasta

2 eggs, beaten

1 1/4 cups strained plain yogurt

2 oz/55 g feta cheese (drained weight), grated

1 oz/25 g romano cheese, grated

salt and pepper

SERVES 6

1 oz/25 g white bread, crusts removed, torn into pieces

2 tbsp milk

1 lb/450 g fresh ground beef

4 tbsp chopped fresh flat-leaf parsley

1 egg

pinch of cayenne pepper

2 tbsp olive oil

$^2/_3$ cup strained canned tomatoes

7 oz/200 g canned chopped tomatoes in juice

$1^3/_4$ cups vegetable stock

pinch of sugar

1 lb/450 g dried spaghetti

salt and pepper

SPAGHETTI AND MEATBALLS

Put the bread in a small bowl, add the milk, and let soak. Meanwhile, put the ground meat in a large bowl and add half the parsley, the egg, and the cayenne pepper. Season to taste with salt and pepper. Squeeze the excess moisture out of the bread and crumble it over the meat mixture. Mix together well until smooth.

Shape small pieces of the mixture into balls between the palms of your hands and put on a cookie sheet or cutting board. Cover and let chill for 30 minutes.

Heat the oil in a heavy-bottomed skillet. Add the meatballs, in batches, and cook, turning frequently, until browned all over. Return all the meatballs to the skillet, add the strained canned tomatoes, tomatoes with their juice, stock, and sugar, and season to taste with salt and pepper. Bring to a boil, stirring, then reduce the heat, cover, and let simmer for 25–30 minutes until the sauce is thickened and the meatballs are tender and cooked through.

Meanwhile, bring a large pan of lightly salted water to a boil. Add the pasta, return to a boil, and cook for 8–10 minutes, or according to the package directions, until tender but still firm to the bite. Drain and transfer to a warmed serving dish. Pour over the sauce and toss lightly. Sprinkle with the remaining parsley and serve.

WHEN FORMING THE MEAT MIXTURE INTO BALLS, DAMPEN YOUR HANDS SLIGHTLY WITH A LITTLE COLD WATER TO HELP PREVENT THE MIXTURE STICKING.

PORK STIR-FRY

Mix the soy sauce, rice wine, vinegar, sugar, and five-spice powder together in a small bowl. Drain the pineapple, reserving the juice in a pitcher. Chop the pineapple and set aside. Stir the cornstarch into the pineapple juice until a smooth paste forms, then stir the paste into the soy sauce mixture and set aside.

Heat the oil in a preheated wok or large, heavy-bottomed skillet over high heat. Add the scallions, garlic, and ginger and stir-fry for 30 seconds. Add the pork strips and stir-fry for 3 minutes, or until browned all over.

Add the carrots, baby corn, and green bell pepper and stir-fry for 3 minutes. Add the bean sprouts and snow peas and stir-fry for 2 minutes. Add the pineapple and the soy sauce mixture and cook, stirring constantly, for another 2 minutes, or until slightly thickened. Transfer to warmed serving bowls and serve immediately.

SERVES 4

2 tbsp dark soy sauce

1 tbsp rice wine or dry sherry

1 tbsp rice vinegar

1 tbsp brown sugar

1 tsp Chinese five-spice powder

8 oz/225 g canned pineapple rings in juice

1 tbsp cornstarch

1 tbsp peanut oil

4 scallions, chopped

1 garlic clove, finely chopped

1-inch/2.5-cm piece fresh gingerroot, finely chopped

12 oz/350 g pork loin, cut into very thin strips

3 carrots, cut into thin sticks

6 oz/175 g baby corn

1 green bell pepper, seeded and thinly sliced

3/4 cup fresh bean sprouts

4 oz/115 g snow peas

LENTILS WITH SAUSAGES

SERVES 4–6

2 tbsp sunflower-seed oil, plus extra for brushing

1 large onion, finely chopped

2 large garlic cloves, finely chopped

2 carrots, cut into ¼-inch/ 5-mm dice

2 cups Puy lentils, rinsed

½ tsp dried thyme

1 bay leaf

4–12 fresh sausages

2 tbsp chopped fresh flat-leaf parsley

salt and pepper

VINAIGRETTE

¼ cup walnut oil

4½ tsp white wine vinegar or lemon juice

½ tsp Dijon mustard

¼ tsp superfine sugar

salt and pepper

To make the vinaigrette, put all ingredients in a jar, then blend using a stick blender until a thick emulsion forms. Alternatively, put all the ingredients in a screw-top jar, secure the lid, and shake vigorously until the emulsion forms. Taste and adjust the seasoning if necessary, and set aside.

Heat the oil in a heavy-bottomed pan with a tight-fitting lid over medium–high heat. Add the onion, garlic, and carrots and cook, stirring frequently, for 5 minutes, or until the onion is softened but not browned.

Stir in the lentils. Add enough water to cover the lentils by 1 inch/2.5 cm and bring to a boil, skimming the surface with a spoon, if necessary. Stir in the thyme and bay leaf, then reduce the heat to low, cover, and let simmer for 10 minutes.

Uncover the pan and simmer for an additional 15–20 minutes, or until the carrots and lentils are tender. If the water is absorbed before the lentils are tender, add a little more and continue cooking.

Meanwhile, preheat the broiler to high. Brush the broiler rack with oil. Lightly prick the sausages all over and cook under the preheated broiler, turning occasionally, until cooked through and the skins are crisp and brown. Set aside and keep warm.

The lentils should absorb all the water by the time they are tender, but if any remains on the surface, drain it off. Transfer the lentils to a large serving bowl. Add the vinaigrette to the hot lentils and stir so that they are well coated.

Add salt and pepper to taste, then stir in the parsley. Serve the hot lentils with the sausages.

GRILLED PORK WITH ORANGE SAUCE

Mix the orange juice, vinegar, and garlic together in a shallow, nonmetallic dish and season to taste with pepper. Add the pork and turn to coat in the marinade. Cover and let marinate in the refrigerator for up to 3 hours.

Meanwhile, mix all the ingredients for the gremolata together in a small bowl, cover, and let chill until required.

Heat a nonstick griddle or grill pan over medium–high heat and brush lightly with oil. Remove the pork from the marinade–reserving the marinade–add to the griddle or grill pan, and cook for 5 minutes on each side, or until cooked through.

Meanwhile, pour the marinade into a small pan, bring to a boil, and boil for 5 minutes, or until slightly thickened.

Transfer the pork to a serving dish, pour the orange sauce over, and sprinkle with the gremolata. Serve immediately.

SERVES 4

4 tbsp freshly squeezed orange juice

4 tbsp red wine vinegar

2 garlic cloves, finely chopped

4 pork steaks, trimmed of all visible fat

olive oil, for brushing

pepper

GREMOLATA

3 tbsp finely chopped fresh parsley

grated rind of 1 lime

grated rind of $^1/_2$ lemon

1 garlic clove, very finely chopped

THIS DISH WOULD WORK EQUALLY WELL WITH CHICKEN BREAST PORTIONS. REMOVE THE SKIN FROM THE COOKED CHICKEN BEFORE SERVING.

SWEET-AND-SOUR GLAZED PORK

Preheat the oven to 450°F/230°C. To make the stuffing, melt the butter in a pan over medium heat. Add the onion and cook, stirring, for 3 minutes, or until slightly softened. Add the mushrooms and cook, stirring, for 2 minutes. Remove from the heat and stir in the bread crumbs, chopped sage, lemon juice, and salt and pepper to taste.

Put the stuffing in the middle of the pork loin, then roll up and secure with several lengths of string tied around the loin. Put the joint in a roasting pan, rub the skin with plenty of salt, and season to taste with pepper. Mix the honey, vinegar, soy sauce, and mustard together in a small bowl. Pour the mixture over the pork.

Cook in the preheated oven for 20 minutes, then reduce the heat to 350°F/180°C and cook, basting occasionally, for 1¼ hours, or until tender and cooked through.

Remove from the oven and let rest for 15 minutes. Garnish with sage sprigs and serve with roasted root vegetables.

SERVES 4

2 lb 4 oz/1 kg pork loin, backbone removed and rind scored

6 tbsp honey

1 tbsp wine vinegar

1 tsp soy sauce

1 tsp Dijon mustard

salt and pepper

roasted root vegetables, to serve

STUFFING

6 tbsp butter

1 onion, chopped

3½ oz/100 g white mushrooms, chopped

1¾ cup fresh bread crumbs

2 tbsp finely chopped fresh sage, plus extra sprigs to garnish

1 tbsp lemon juice

salt and pepper

KIDNEYS IN MUSTARD SAUCE

Using a pair of kitchen scissors, remove the cores from the kidneys and discard. Melt the butter with the oil in a large sauté pan or skillet over medium–high heat. Add the kidney halves, in batches if necessary, and cook, turning occasionally, for 3 minutes, or until browned all over. Using a slotted spoon, transfer the kidneys to a plate, cover with foil, shiny-side down, set aside, and keep warm.

Add the shallots and garlic to the pan and cook for 2 minutes, or until the shallots are softened but not browned. Add the wine, bring to a boil, and boil until reduced by half,

scraping the sediment from the bottom of the pan.

Add the stock, return to a boil, and boil again until reduced by half. Stir in the cream and mustard, reduce the heat to medium–low, and return the kidneys to the pan. Cover and simmer for 5 minutes, or until the kidneys are cooked.

Remove the kidneys from the pan and keep warm. Increase the heat under the sauce and let bubble until reduced and thickened.

Add salt and pepper to taste, return the kidneys to the pan, and stir well. Garnish with chopped parsley and serve immediately.

SERVES 4–6

12 lamb's kidneys, skinned and halved

2 tbsp unsalted butter

1 tbsp sunflower-seed oil

2 large shallots, chopped

1 garlic clove, very finely chopped

2 tbsp dry white wine

$1/2$ cup chicken or lamb stock

generous 1 cup heavy cream

2 tbsp Dijon mustard, or to taste

salt and pepper

chopped fresh flat-leaf parsley, to garnish

LAMB'S LIVER IN RED WINE AND ORANGE SAUCE

Using a zester, remove the zest from the oranges. Put the zest in a small pan of boiling water, boil for 1 minute, then drain and set aside. Squeeze the juice from the oranges and set aside.

Remove and discard any ducts and membrane from the liver slices. Put the flour and paprika in a plastic bag, add the liver, and shake well to coat each piece.

Heat the oil in a large skillet over medium heat. Add the liver and cook, stirring constantly, for 4–5 minutes until lightly browned all over but still moist in the center.

Remove from the skillet with a slotted spoon and divide between 4 warmed serving plates on a bed of cooked pasta.

Add the wine to the skillet, scraping any sediment from the bottom of the pan. Boil briskly for 1 minute. Reduce the heat and stir in the orange juice, parsley, oregano, and salt and pepper to taste. Cook gently until slightly reduced, then spoon over the liver and garnish with the reserved orange zest and parsley. Serve immediately.

SERVES 4

2 oranges

8 thin slices lamb's or calf's liver

2 tbsp all-purpose flour

1 tsp paprika

3 tbsp olive oil

³/₄ cup full-bodied red wine

2 tbsp chopped fresh flat-leaf parsley, plus extra to garnish

2 tbsp chopped fresh oregano

salt and pepper

cooked pasta, to serve

LAMB AND MINT BURGERS

Preheat the broiler to medium. Put the bell peppers, onion, and eggplant on the broiler rack, brush the eggplant with 1 tablespoon of the oil, and cook under the broiler for 10–12 minutes, or until charred. Remove from the broiler, let cool, then peel the bell peppers. Put all the vegetables in a food processor and pulse until chopped.

Add the lamb, Parmesan cheese, mint, and salt and pepper to taste to the food processor and process until the mixture comes together.

Scrape onto a cutting board. With damp hands, shape the mixture into 4–6 equal-size burgers. Cover and let chill for at least 30 minutes.

Mix together the mayonnaise ingredients. Preheat the broiler to medium. Lightly brush the burgers with the remaining oil and cook under the broiler for 3–4 minutes on each side. Serve the burgers on a bed of lettuce on the bases of the buns. Spoon the mayonnaise on top of each burger and place the lids in position.

SERVES 4–6

1 red bell pepper, seeded and cut into quarters

1 yellow bell pepper, seeded and cut into quarters

1 red onion, cut into thick wedges

1 baby eggplant, about 4 oz/ 115 g, cut into wedges

2 tbsp olive oil

1 lb/450 g fresh ground lamb

2 tbsp freshly grated Parmesan cheese

1 tbsp chopped fresh mint

salt and pepper

MAYONNAISE

4 tbsp mayonnaise

1 tsp Dijon mustard

1 tbsp chopped fresh mint

TO SERVE

4–6 toasted sesame seed buns

lettuce leaves, shredded

LAMB MEATBALLS

Put the ground lamb in a bowl. Add the onion, garlic, bread crumbs, mint, and parsley. Season well with salt and pepper. Mix the ingredients together well, then add the egg and mix to bind the mixture together. Alternatively, place the ingredients in a food processor and process until combined.

Preheat the broiler to medium. With damp hands, shape the mixture into 16 equal-size balls and thread onto 4 flat metal skewers.

Lightly oil a broiler pan and brush the meatballs with oil.

Cook the meatballs under the preheated broiler, turning frequently and brushing with more oil if necessary, for 10 minutes, or until cooked through and browned.

SERVES 4

1 lb/450 g fine lean fresh ground lamb

1 onion, grated

1 garlic clove, crushed

$^1/_2$ cup fresh white or brown bread crumbs

1 tbsp chopped fresh mint

1 tbsp chopped fresh parsley

1 egg, beaten

olive oil, for brushing

salt and pepper

LAMB SHANKS WITH ROASTED ONIONS

Preheat the oven to 350°F/180°C. Trim off any excess fat from the lamb shanks. Using a small, sharp knife, make 6 cuts in each. Cut the garlic cloves lengthwise into 4 slices. Insert 6 garlic slices into the cuts in each lamb shank.

Put the lamb in a single layer in a roasting pan, drizzle with the oil, sprinkle with the rosemary, and season to taste with pepper. Roast in the preheated oven for 45 minutes.

Wrap each of the onions in a piece of foil. Remove the roasting pan from the oven and season the lamb to taste with salt. Return to the oven and put the wrapped onions on the shelf next to it. Roast for an additional 1–1$\frac{1}{4}$ hours until the lamb is very tender.

Meanwhile, bring a large pan of water to a boil. Add the carrot sticks and blanch for 1 minute. Drain and refresh in cold water.

Remove the roasting pan from the oven when the lamb is meltingly tender and transfer to a warmed serving dish. Skim off any fat from the roasting pan and put the pan over medium heat. Add the carrots and cook, stirring, for 2 minutes, then add the water and bring to a boil. Reduce the heat and simmer, stirring constantly and scraping any sediment from the bottom of the pan.

Transfer the carrots and sauce to the serving dish. Remove the onions from the oven and unwrap. Cut off and discard about $\frac{1}{2}$ inch/1 cm of the tops and add the onions to the serving dish. Serve immediately.

SERVES 4

4 lamb shanks, about 12 oz/ 350 g each

6 garlic cloves

2 tbsp extra virgin olive oil

1 tbsp fresh rosemary, very finely chopped

4 red onions

12 oz/350 g carrots, cut into thin sticks

4 tbsp water

salt and pepper

5

ROASTS

Few meals are more satisfying than a good roast. The age-old ritual of carving a roast for family and friends is the epitome of the meat-eating tradition, incorporating a sociable occasion with the taste of traditional comfort food. Roasting is the easiest way of cooking meat, but it does call for top-quality produce, and it's absolutely vital to let the meat rest for at least 15 minutes before carving it—the meat will be juicier and more tender as a result. You'll find ideas for roasting all types of meat, poultry or game, including Roast Pork with Crackling, Roast Turkey with Bread Sauce, and Quails with Grapes, or you can try out a new take on an old favorite, such as Roast Chicken Breasts with Bread Triangles or Roast Lamb with Orzo.

ROAST CHICKEN

SERVES 6

1 free-range chicken, weighing
5 lb/2.25 kg

4 tbsp butter

2 tbsp chopped fresh lemon
thyme, plus 6 extra sprigs
to garnish

1 lemon, quartered

$^1/_2$ cup dry white wine, plus
extra, if required

salt and pepper

Preheat the oven to 425°F/220°C.
Wipe the chicken inside and out
with paper towels and put in a
roasting pan.

Put the butter in a bowl and
soften with a fork, then mix in the
thyme and season well with salt
and pepper. Spread the chicken all
over with the herb butter, inside
and out, and put the lemon quarters
inside the body cavity. Pour $^1/_2$ cup
wine over the chicken.

Roast the chicken in the center of
the preheated oven for 20 minutes.
Reduce the temperature to

375°F/190°C and roast, basting
frequently, for an additional
$1^1/_4$ hours, or until tender and the
juices run clear when a skewer is
inserted into the thickest part of
the meat. Cover with foil if the skin
begins to brown too much. If the
roasting pan begins to dry out, add
a little more wine or water.

Transfer the chicken to a warmed
serving plate and let rest, covered
loosely with foil, for at least
15 minutes before carving.

Put the roasting pan on the stove
over low heat and cook the pan
juices until reduced, thickened, and
glossy. Season to taste with salt
and pepper.

Serve the roast chicken with the
pan juices, garnished with the
lemon thyme sprigs.

SIMPLY ROASTED, WITH LOTS OF THYME AND LEMON,
CHICKEN PRODUCES A SUCCULENT GASTRONOMIC
FEAST FOR MANY OCCASIONS. TRY TO BUY A GOOD
FRESH CHICKEN, AS FROZEN BIRDS DO NOT HAVE AS
MUCH FLAVOR. YOU CAN STUFF YOUR CHICKEN WITH
A TRADITIONAL STUFFING, SUCH AS SAGE AND
ONION, OR FRUIT SUCH AS APRICOTS AND PRUNES,
BUT OFTEN THE BEST WAY IS TO KEEP IT SIMPLE.

ROAST CHICKEN BREASTS WITH BREAD TRIANGLES

Preheat the oven to 400°F/200°C. Melt the butter in a pan over medium heat, add the lemon juice, cranberries, sugar, and salt and pepper to taste. Cook, stirring gently, for 1 minute and let cool until required.

Meanwhile, season the chicken to taste with salt and pepper. Wrap 2 bacon strips around each breast and sprinkle with thyme.

Wrap each breast in a piece of lightly greased foil and put in a roasting pan. Roast in the preheated oven for 15 minutes. Remove the foil and roast the chicken breasts for an additional 10 minutes.

Heat the drippings in a skillet over medium–high heat. Add the bread triangles and cook on both sides until golden brown.

Put a fried bread triangle on each individual warmed serving plate and top each with a chicken breast.

Serve immediately with a spoonful of the fruit sauce.

SERVES 8

4 tbsp butter, plus extra for greasing

juice of 1 lemon

9 oz/250 g cranberries or red currants

1–2 tbsp brown sugar

8 skinless chicken breasts

16 lean bacon strips

4 tsp dried thyme

$^1/_4$ cup beef drippings

4 slices bread, cut into triangles

salt and pepper

QUAILS WITH GRAPES

Preheat the oven to 450°F/230°C. Cook the potatoes for the crêpe in a large pan of lightly salted water for 10 minutes until partially cooked. Drain and let cool completely, then peel, grate coarsely, and season to taste with salt and pepper. Set aside.

Heat the oil in a heavy-bottomed skillet or ovenproof casserole large enough to hold the quails in a single layer over medium heat. Add the quails and cook, turning frequently, until golden brown all over.

Add the grapes, grape juice, cloves, enough water to come halfway up the sides of the quails, and salt and pepper to taste. Cover and simmer for 20 minutes. Transfer the quails and all the pan juices to a roasting pan, unless using a casserole, and sprinkle with brandy. Roast, uncovered, in the preheated oven for 10 minutes. Meanwhile, to make the potato crêpe, melt the butter with the oil in a 12-inch/30-cm nonstick skillet over high heat. When the fat is hot, add the potato and spread into an even layer. Reduce the heat and cook gently for 10 minutes.

Put a plate over the skillet and, wearing oven mitts, invert both together so that the potato crêpe drops onto the plate. Slide the potato back into the skillet and cook for an additional 10 minutes, or until cooked through and crisp. Slide out of the skillet and cut into 4 wedges. Keep warm until the quails are ready.

To serve, put a potato crêpe wedge and 2 quails on each warmed serving plate. Taste the grape sauce and adjust the seasoning, if necessary. Spoon over the quails and serve immediately.

SERVES 4

4 tbsp olive oil

8 oven-ready quails

10 oz/280 g green seedless grapes

1 cup grape juice

2 cloves

about ²⁄₃ cup water

2 tbsp brandy

salt and pepper

POTATO CRÊPE

1 lb 5 oz/600 g unpeeled potatoes

2¹⁄₂ tbsp unsalted butter or pork fat

1¹⁄₂ tbsp olive oil

BONED AND STUFFED ROAST DUCKLING

Preheat the oven to 375°F/190°C. Wipe the duckling inside and out with paper towels. Lay, skin-side down, on a cutting board and season well with salt and pepper.

Mix the sausage meat, onion, apple, apricots, walnuts, and parsley together in a bowl. Season well with salt and pepper. Form into a large sausage shape.

Lay the duck breast(s) on the whole duckling and cover with the stuffing. Wrap the duckling around the stuffing and carefully tuck in any leg and neck flaps. Sew the duckling up the back and across both ends with fine string. Try to use one piece of string so that you can remove it in one go. Mold the duckling into a good shape and put, sewn-side down, on a cooling rack set over a roasting pan.

Roast in the preheated oven, basting occasionally and pouring off some of the fat in the pan, for 1½–2 hours until golden brown and crisp and the juices run clear when a skewer is inserted into the thickest part of the meat.

Simmer all the sauce ingredients in a pan for 2–3 minutes. Serve with the thickly sliced duck.

SERVES 6–8

1 duckling, weighing 4 lb/1.8 kg (dressed weight); ask your butcher to bone the duckling and cut off the wings at the first joint

1 lb/450 g herb-flavored sausage meat

1 small onion, finely chopped

1 apple, cored and finely chopped

½ cup no-soak dried apricots, finely chopped

½ cup chopped walnuts

2 tbsp chopped fresh parsley

1 large or 2 smaller duck breasts, skin removed

salt and pepper

APRICOT SAUCE

14 oz/400 g canned apricot halves in syrup, puréed with the syrup in a food processor or blender

⅔ cup stock

½ cup Marsala

½ tsp ground cinnamon

½ tsp ground ginger

salt and pepper

GUINEA FOWL WITH CABBAGE

Preheat the oven to 475°F/240°C. Rub the guinea fowl with the oil and season to taste inside and out with salt and pepper. Put the apple and parsley sprigs in the cavity and truss to tie the legs together. Put in a roasting pan and roast in the preheated oven for 20 minutes, or until the breast is golden brown. Immediately reduce the temperature to 325°F/160°C.

Meanwhile, blanch the cabbage in boiling water for 3 minutes. Drain, rinse in cold water, and pat dry.

Put the lardons in an ovenproof casserole over medium–high heat and cook until the fat runs. Remove with a slotted spoon and set aside.

Add the onion and cook, stirring frequently, for 5 minutes, or until softened but not browned. Add the bouquet garni with a very little salt and a pinch of pepper, then return the lardons to the casserole with the cabbage. Top with the guinea fowl. Cover with a piece of wet waxed paper, then add the lid and cook in the preheated oven for 45–60 minutes, or until the guinea fowl is tender and the juices run clear when a skewer is inserted into the thickest part of the meat.

Cut the guinea fowl into portions. Stir the parsley into the cabbage and onion and serve with the meat.

SERVES 4

1 oven-ready guinea fowl, weighing 2 lb 12 oz/1.25 kg

$^1\!/_2$ tbsp sunflower-seed oil

$^1\!/_2$ apple, peeled, cored, and chopped

several fresh flat-leaf parsley sprigs, stems bruised

1 large savoy cabbage, coarse outer leaves discarded, cored, and quartered

1 thick piece smoked belly of pork (side pork), about 5 oz/140 g, rind removed, cut into thin lardons, or 5 oz/140 g unsmoked lardons

1 onion, sliced

1 bouquet garni

$1^1\!/_2$ tbsp chopped fresh flat-leaf parsley

salt and pepper

IT IS IMPORTANT NOT TO ADD TOO MUCH SALT AS THE LARDONS WILL BE SALTY.

ROAST PHEASANT WITH RED WINE AND HERBS

SERVES 4

7 tbsp butter, slightly softened

1 tbsp chopped fresh thyme

1 tbsp chopped fresh parsley

2 oven-ready young pheasants

4 tbsp vegetable oil

$^1/_2$ cup full-bodied red wine

salt and pepper

good-quality, hand-fried chips, to garnish

selection of vegetables, to serve

Preheat the oven to 375°F/190°C. Put the butter in a bowl and soften with a fork, then mix in the herbs. Lift the skins away from the pheasants, taking care not to tear them, and push the herb butter under the skins. Season to taste all over with salt and pepper.

Pour the oil into a roasting pan, add the pheasants, and roast in the preheated oven for 45 minutes, basting occasionally. Remove from the oven, pour over the wine, then return to the oven and roast for another 15 minutes, or until tender and the juices run clear when a skewer is inserted into the thickest part of the meat of both birds.

Remove the pheasants from the oven, cover loosely with foil, and let rest for 15 minutes.

Transfer to a warmed serving platter and garnish with the chips, known as game chips. To serve, cut the pheasants into portions and accompany with vegetables.

CHRISTMAS GOOSE WITH HONEY AND PEARS

SERVES 4

1 oven-ready goose, weighing
7 lb 12 oz–10 lb/3.5–4.5 kg

1 tsp salt

4 pears

1 tbsp lemon juice

4 tbsp butter

2 tbsp honey

selection of vegetables, to serve

Preheat the oven to 425°F/220°C. Rinse the goose and pat dry with paper towels. Prick the skin all over with a fork, then rub with the salt. Put the bird upside down on a rack set over a roasting pan. Roast in the preheated oven for 30 minutes. Drain off the fat. Turn the bird over and roast for another 15 minutes. Drain off the fat. Reduce the temperature to 350°F/180°C. Roast for an additional 15 minutes per 1 lb/450 g, or until the juices run clear when a skewer is inserted into the thickest part of the meat. Cover with foil 15 minutes before the end of the cooking time.

Peel and halve the pears and brush with the lemon juice. Melt the butter and honey in a pan over low heat, then add the pears. Cook, stirring, for 5–10 minutes until tender. Arrange around the goose on a serving platter and pour the sweet juices over the bird. Serve with a selection of vegetables.

GOOSE FAT IS SIMPLY PERFECT FOR ROASTING (AND SAUTÉEING) POTATOES, SO DON'T WASTE IT. POUR ANY THAT YOU ARE NOT ABOUT TO USE IMMEDIATELY INTO A SCREW-TOP JAR AND STORE IN THE REFRIGERATOR.

ROAST TURKEY WITH BREAD SAUCE

SERVES 8

1 quantity Chestnut and Sausage Stuffing

1 turkey, weighing 11 lb/5 kg

4 tbsp butter

5 tbsp full-bodied red wine

1³/₄ cups chicken stock

1 tbsp cornstarch

1 tsp French mustard

1 tsp sherry vinegar

2 teaspoons water

BREAD SAUCE

1 onion, peeled

4 cloves

2¹/₂ cups milk

2 cups fresh white bread crumbs

4 tbsp butter

salt and pepper

Preheat the oven to 425°F/220°C. Spoon the stuffing into the neck cavity of the turkey and close the flap of skin with a skewer. Put the bird in a large roasting pan and rub all over with 3 tablespoons of the butter. Roast in the preheated oven for 1 hour, then reduce the temperature to 350°F/180°C and roast for an additional 2¹/₂ hours, or until tender and the juices run clear when a skewer is inserted into the thickest part of the meat. You may need to pour off the fat from the roasting pan occasionally.

Meanwhile, to make the bread sauce, stud the onion with the cloves, then put in a pan with the milk, bread crumbs, and butter. Bring just to boiling point over low heat, then remove from the heat and let stand in a warm place to infuse.

Just before serving, remove the onion and reheat the sauce over low heat, beating well with a wooden spoon. Season to taste with salt and pepper.

When the turkey is cooked, transfer to a carving board, cover loosely with foil, and let rest.

To make the gravy, skim off the fat from the roasting pan, then place the pan over medium heat. Add the wine and stir, scraping the sediment from the bottom of the pan. Stir in the stock. Mix the cornstarch, mustard, vinegar, and water together in a small bowl, then stir into the pan. Bring to a boil, stirring constantly, and cook until thickened and smooth. Add the remaining butter.

Carve the turkey and serve with the warm bread sauce.

ROAST PORK WITH CRACKLING

Preheat the oven to 400°F/200°C.

Score the pork rind thoroughly with a sharp knife and sprinkle with salt. Put it on a cooling rack set over a cookie sheet and roast in the preheated oven for 30–40 minutes until the crackling is golden brown and crisp. This can be cooked in advance, leaving room in the oven for roast potatoes.

Season the pork well with salt and pepper and spread the fat with the mustard. Put in a roasting pan and roast in the center of the oven for 20 minutes. Reduce the temperature to 375°F/190°C and cook for an additional 50–60 minutes until the meat is well browned and the juices run clear when a skewer is inserted into the thickest part of the meat.

Remove the meat from the oven and transfer to a warmed serving plate, cover loosely with foil, and leave in a warm place to rest.

Meanwhile, to make the apple sauce, put all the ingredients into a pan over low heat. Cook for 10 minutes, stirring occasionally. Beat well until the sauce is thick and smooth—use a hand-held electric whisk for a smooth finish, if necessary.

To make the gravy, pour off most of the fat from the roasting pan, leaving the meat juices and the sediment. Put the pan over medium heat and scrape the sediment from the bottom of the pan. Sprinkle in the flour and quickly whisk it into the juices. When you have a smooth paste, gradually add the cider, whisking constantly. Bring to a boil, then reduce the heat and simmer for 2–3 minutes until thickened. Season well with salt and pepper and pour into a warmed serving pitcher.

Carve the pork into slices and serve on warmed plates with pieces of the crackling and the gravy. Accompany with the apple sauce.

SERVES 4

1 boned pork loin joint, weighing 2 lb 4 oz/1 kg, rind removed and set aside

2 tbsp mustard

salt and pepper

APPLE SAUCE

1 lb/450 g cooking apples, peeled, cored and sliced

3 tablespoons water

1 tbsp superfine sugar

pinch of ground cinnamon (optional)

1 tbsp butter (optional)

GRAVY

1 tbsp flour

1¼ cups cider, apple juice, or chicken stock

salt and pepper

GLAZED HAM

Put the ham in a large pan and add enough cold water to cover. Bring to a boil and skim off the scum that rises to the surface. Reduce the heat and simmer for 30 minutes.

Drain the ham and return to the pan. Add the apple, onion, cider, peppercorns, bouquet garni, bay leaf, and a few of the cloves. Pour in enough fresh water to cover and return to a boil. Reduce the heat, cover, and let simmer for 3 hours 20 minutes.

Preheat the oven to 400°F/200°C. Remove from the heat and let cool slightly, before removing from the cooking liquid. While the ham is still warm, loosen the rind with a sharp knife, peel it off, and discard. Score the fat into diamond shapes and stud with the remaining cloves. Put the ham on a rack, over a roasting pan, and sprinkle with the sugar. Roast in the preheated oven, basting occasionally with the cooking liquid, for 20 minutes. Serve hot or cold.

SERVES 8

1 ham joint, weighing
9 lb/4 kg

1 apple, cored and chopped

1 onion, chopped

1^1/$_4$ cups cider

6 black peppercorns

1 bouquet garni

1 bay leaf

about 50 cloves

4 tbsp raw brown sugar

PORK WITH RED CABBAGE

Preheat the oven to 325°F/160°C. Heat the oil in an ovenproof casserole over medium heat. Add the pork and cook until browned all over. Transfer to a plate.

Add the onion and cook over low heat, stirring occasionally, for 5 minutes, or until softened. Add the cabbage, in batches, and cook, stirring, for 2 minutes. Transfer each batch (mixed with some onion) into a bowl with a slotted spoon.

Add the apples, cloves, and sugar to the bowl and mix well. Put about half the mixture in the bottom of the casserole. Top with the pork and add the remaining cabbage mixture. Sprinkle in the lemon juice and add the strip of rind. Cover and cook in the preheated oven for 1½ hours.

Transfer the pork to a plate. Transfer the cabbage mixture to the plate with a slotted spoon and keep warm. Bring the cooking juices to a boil and reduce slightly. Serve the pork in slices with the cabbage mixture. Spoon over the cooking juices. Garnish with lemon wedges.

SERVES 4

1 tbsp sunflower-seed oil

1 boned and rolled pork loin joint, weighing 1 lb 10 oz/750 g

1 onion, finely chopped

1 lb 2 oz/500 g red cabbage, thick stems discarded and leaves shredded

2 large cooking apples, peeled, cored, and sliced

3 cloves

1 tsp brown sugar

3 tbsp lemon juice

thinly pared strip of lemon rind

lemon wedges, to garnish

SLOW-ROASTED PORK

Preheat the oven to 300°F/150°C.

Using a small, sharp knife, cut slits all over the pork, opening them out slightly to make little pockets.

Put the garlic slices in a small strainer and rinse under cold running water to moisten. Spread the fennel out on a saucer and roll the garlic slices in it to coat.

Slide the garlic slices and the cloves into the pockets in the pork. Season the meat all over with salt and pepper.

Put the pork in a large ovenproof dish or roasting pan. Pour in the wine and water. Roast in the preheated oven, basting occasionally, for 2$^{1}/_{2}$–2$^{3}/_{4}$ hours, until the pork is tender but still quite moist.

If you are serving the pork hot, transfer it to a carving board and cut into slices. If you are serving it cold, let it cool completely in the cooking juices before removing and slicing.

SERVES 6

1 boned and rolled pork loin joint, weighing 3 lb 8 oz/1.6 kg

4 garlic cloves, thinly sliced lengthwise

1$^{1}/_{2}$ tsp finely chopped fresh fennel fronds or $^{1}/_{2}$ tsp dried fennel

4 cloves

1$^{1}/_{4}$ cups dry white wine

1$^{1}/_{4}$ cups water

salt and pepper

ROAST VENISON WITH BRANDY SAUCE

Preheat the oven to 350°F/180°C.

Heat half the oil in a skillet over high heat. Season the venison to taste with salt and pepper, add to the skillet and cook until lightly browned all over.

Pour the remaining oil into a roasting pan. Add the venison, cover with foil, and roast in the preheated oven, basting occasionally, for 1 1/2 hours, or until cooked through. Remove from the oven and transfer to a warmed serving platter. Cover loosely with foil and let rest.

To make the sauce, stir the flour into the roasting pan over medium heat and cook, stirring constantly, for 1 minute. Stir in the stock, scraping the sediment from the bottom of the pan. Gradually stir in the brandy and bring to a boil, then reduce the heat and simmer, stirring frequently, for 10 minutes, or until the sauce has thickened a little. Remove from the heat and stir in the cream.

Garnish the venison with thyme sprigs and serve with the brandy sauce and a selection of vegetables.

SERVES 4

6 tbsp vegetable oil

1 saddle of fresh venison, weighing 3 lb 12 oz/1.7 kg, trimmed

salt and pepper

fresh thyme sprigs, to garnish

selection of vegetables, to serve

BRANDY SAUCE

1 tbsp all-purpose flour

4 tbsp vegetable stock

3/4 cup brandy

generous 1/3 cup heavy cream

BOTH WILD AND FARMED VENISON IS SURPRISINGLY INEXPENSIVE COMPARED WITH LAMB OR BEEF. IT MAY BE FRESH OR FROZEN. VENISON HAS A DELICATE TEXTURE AND IS HIGH IN PROTEIN BUT LOW IN FAT, SO IT IS VERY NUTRITIOUS.

SERVES 6

1 leg of lamb, weighing
3 lb 5 oz/1.5 kg

6 garlic cloves, thinly sliced
lengthwise

8 fresh rosemary sprigs

4 tbsp olive oil

salt and pepper

GLAZE

4 tbsp red currant jelly

1¼ cups rosé wine

ROAST LAMB WITH GARLIC AND ROSEMARY

Preheat the oven to 400°F/200°C.
Using a small, sharp knife, cut slits
all over the leg of lamb. Insert
1–2 garlic slices and 4–5 rosemary
needles into each slit. Put any
remaining rosemary in the bottom
of a roasting pan. Season the lamb
to taste with salt and pepper and
put in the roasting pan. Pour over
the oil. Cover with foil and roast
in the preheated oven for 1 hour
20 minutes.

To make the glaze, mix the red
currant jelly and wine together in
a small pan. Heat over low heat,
stirring constantly, until combined.
Bring to a boil, then reduce the heat
and simmer until reduced. Remove
the lamb from the oven and pour
over the glaze. Return to the oven
and roast, uncovered, for about
10 minutes, depending on how well
done you like it.

Remove the lamb from the
roasting pan and transfer to a
carving board. Cover loosely with
foil and let rest for 15 minutes
before carving and serving.

ROAST LAMB WITH ORZO

Preheat the oven to 350°F/180°C.

Untie the lamb and open out. Arrange the lemon slices down the center and sprinkle over half the oregano, the chopped garlic, and salt and pepper to taste. Roll up the meat and tie with string. Cut slits all over the lamb and insert a garlic slice into each slit.

Put the tomatoes with their juice, cold water, remaining oregano, the sugar, and bay leaf in a large roasting pan. Put the lamb on top, drizzle over the oil, and season to taste with salt and pepper.

Roast the lamb in the preheated oven for 1 hour 5 minutes. 15 minutes before the end of the cooking time, stir the boiling water and orzo into the tomatoes in the pan. Add a little extra water if the sauce seems too thick. Return to the oven for an additional 15 minutes, or until the lamb and orzo are tender and the tomatoes are reduced to a thick sauce.

To serve, carve the lamb into slices and serve hot with the orzo and tomato sauce.

SERVES 4

1 boned leg or shoulder of lamb, weighing 1 lb 10 oz/ 750 g

$\frac{1}{2}$ lemon, thinly sliced

1 tbsp chopped fresh oregano

4 large garlic cloves, 2 finely chopped and 2 thinly sliced

1 lb 12 oz/800 g canned chopped tomatoes in juice

$\frac{2}{3}$ cup cold water

pinch of sugar

1 bay leaf

2 tbsp olive oil

$\frac{2}{3}$ cup boiling water

generous 1 cup dried orzo or short-grain rice

salt and pepper

ORZO IS A VERY SMALL FORM OF PASTA THAT LOOKS LIKE FLAT WHEAT GRAINS. IT IS USED IN SOUP AND MEAT DISHES AND SERVED AS AN ACCOMPANIMENT. IN THIS RECIPE IT IS BAKED WITH LAMB AND ABSORBS THE MEAT JUICES, GIVING IT THE MOST WONDERFUL FLAVOR.

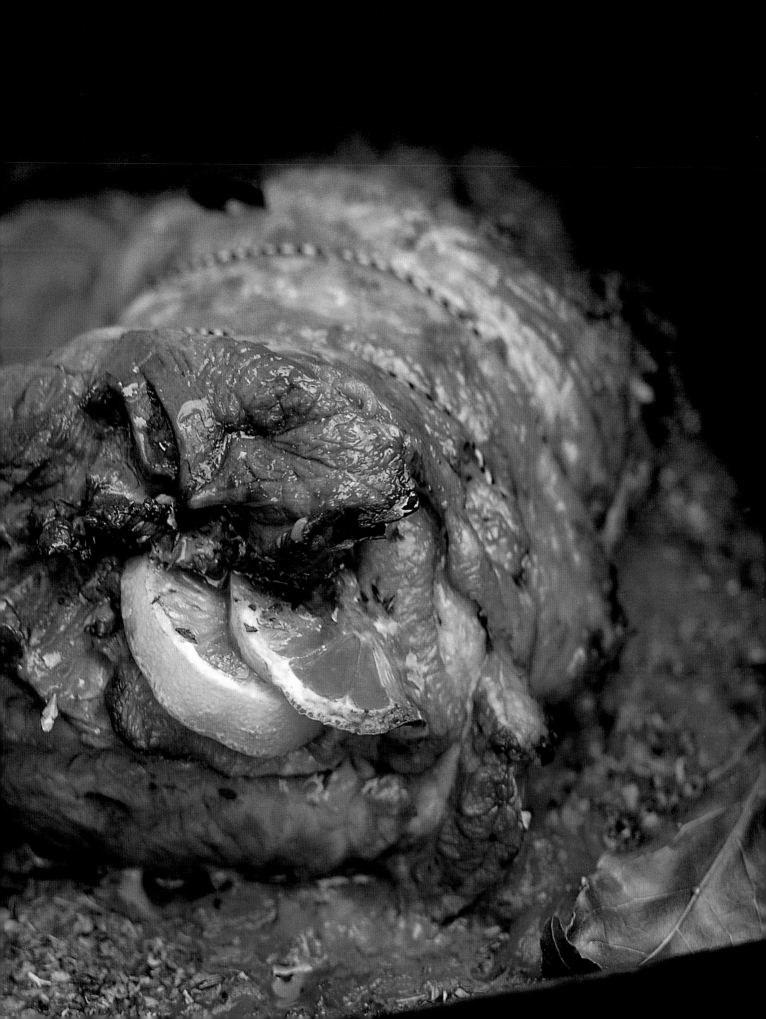

POT ROASTED LEG OF LAMB

SERVES 4

1 leg of lamb, weighing
3 lb 8 oz/1.6 kg

3–4 fresh rosemary sprigs

4 oz/115 g lean bacon slices

4 tbsp olive oil

2–3 garlic cloves, crushed

2 onions, sliced

2 carrots, sliced

2 celery stalks, sliced

1¼ cups dry white wine

1 tbsp tomato paste

1¼ cups lamb or chicken stock

3 medium tomatoes, peeled,
quartered, and seeded

1 tbsp chopped fresh parsley

1 tbsp chopped fresh oregano
or marjoram

salt and pepper

fresh rosemary sprigs,
to garnish

Preheat the oven to 325°F/160°C.

Wipe the lamb all over with paper towels, trim off any excess fat, and season to taste with salt and pepper, rubbing in well. Lay the sprigs of rosemary over the lamb, cover evenly with the bacon slices, and tie securely in place with kitchen string.

Heat the oil in a skillet and pan-fry the lamb over medium heat for 10 minutes, turning several times. Remove from the skillet. Transfer the oil to a large ovenproof casserole and cook the garlic and onions for 3–4 minutes until the onions are starting to soften. Add the carrots and celery and cook for an additional few minutes.

Lay the lamb on top of the vegetables and press down to partly submerge. Pour the wine over the lamb, add the tomato paste, and let simmer for 3–4 minutes. Add the stock, tomatoes, and herbs and season to taste with salt and pepper. Return to a boil for 3–4 minutes. Cover the casserole tightly and cook in the oven for 2–2½ hours until very tender.

Remove the lamb from the casserole and remove the bacon and herbs together with the string. Keep the lamb warm. Strain the juices, skimming off any excess fat, and serve in a pitcher. The vegetables may be put around the joint or in a dish. Garnish with rosemary sprigs.

BEEF POT ROAST WITH POTATOES AND DILL

SERVES 6

2¹/₂ tbsp all-purpose flour

1 tsp salt

¹/₄ tsp pepper

1 rolled brisket joint, weighing
3 lb 8 oz/1.6 kg

2 tbsp vegetable oil

2 tbsp butter

1 onion, finely chopped

2 celery stalks, diced

2 carrots, diced

1 tsp dill seed

1 tsp dried thyme or oregano

1¹/₂ cups full-bodied
red wine

²/₃–1 cup beef stock

4–5 potatoes, cut into large
chunks and boiled until
just tender

2 tbsp chopped fresh dill,
to garnish

Preheat the oven to 275°F/140°C.

Mix 2 tablespoons of the flour with the salt and pepper in a shallow dish. Dip the meat into the mixture to coat. Heat the oil in an ovenproof casserole. Add the brisket and cook until browned all over. Transfer to a plate.

Melt half the butter in the casserole over medium heat. Add the onion, celery, carrots, dill seed, and thyme and cook, stirring frequently, for 5 minutes. Return the meat and juices to the casserole.

Pour in the wine and enough stock to reach one-third of the way up the meat. Bring to a boil, then reduce the heat, cover, and cook in the preheated oven for 3 hours, turning the meat every 30 minutes. After the meat has been cooking for 2 hours, add the potatoes and more stock, if necessary.

When ready, transfer the meat and vegetables to a warmed serving dish. Strain the cooking liquid into a pan.

Mix the remaining butter and flour to a paste. Bring the cooking liquid to a boil. Whisk in small pieces of the flour and butter paste, whisking constantly until the sauce is smooth. Pour the sauce over the meat and vegetables. Sprinkle with the fresh dill and serve immediately.

ROAST BEEF

SERVES 8

1 prime rib of beef, weighing
6 lb/2.7 kg

2 tsp English mustard powder

3 tbsp all-purpose flour

1¼ cups full-bodied red wine

1¼ cups beef stock

2 tsp Worcestershire sauce
(optional)

salt and pepper

Preheat the oven to 450°F/230°C.

Season the rib of beef to taste with salt and pepper and rub in the mustard and 1 tablespoon of the flour.

Put the meat in a roasting pan large enough to hold it comfortably and roast in the preheated oven for 15 minutes. Reduce the heat to 375°F/190°C and cook for 1 hour 45 minutes for rare beef or 2 hours 20 minutes for medium beef. Baste the meat occasionally to keep it moist. If the pan becomes too dry, add a little stock or red wine.

When the meat is cooked, transfer to a warmed serving plate, cover loosely with foil, and let rest for 10–15 minutes.

To make the gravy, put the roasting pan over medium heat and scrape the sediment from the bottom of the pan. Sprinkle in the remaining flour and quickly whisk it into the juices. When you have a smooth paste, gradually add the wine and most of the stock, whisking constantly. Bring to a boil, then reduce the heat and cook for 2–3 minutes until thickened. Season to taste with salt and pepper, add the remaining stock, if necessary, and add a little Worcestershire sauce, if you like.

When ready to serve, carve the meat into slices and serve on warmed plates. Pour the gravy into a warmed pitcher to serve.

6

CASSEROLES
AND STEWS

Meat's versatility and diversity really comes into its own when it comes to casseroles and stews. In this chapter you'll find a whole range of eating experiences, from the spicy to the smooth, with numerous delicious stops along the way. There are many international favorites here, such as Lamb Tagine, Veal with Gremolata, Lone Star Chili, and Beef Casserole, or you might like to try something new, such as Rabbit with Prunes or Beef Stew with Olives.

CHICKEN, SAUSAGE, AND BEAN STEW

Heat the oil in a large, heavy-bottomed pan over medium–high heat. Add the chicken, pork sausage, and frankfurters and cook until lightly browned all over. Reduce the heat to medium. Add the onion and carrots and cook, stirring frequently, for 5 minutes, or until softened.

Stir in the garlic, thyme, and red pepper flakes and cook, stirring, for 1 minute. Stir in the tomatoes with their juice, beans, and stock. Season to taste with salt and pepper. Bring to a boil, then reduce the heat and simmer over low heat, stirring occasionally, for 20–30 minutes.

Garnish with chopped parsley just before serving.

SERVES 4

2 tbsp vegetable oil

4 boneless, skinless chicken breasts, about 4 oz/115 g each, cubed

8 oz/225 g coarse-textured pork sausage, cut into large chunks

4 frankfurter sausages, halved

1 onion, finely chopped

3 carrots, thinly sliced

1 garlic clove, very finely chopped

1 tsp dried thyme

$1/4$–$1/2$ tsp red pepper flakes

14 oz/400 g canned chopped tomatoes in juice

14 oz/400 g canned cannellini beans, drained and rinsed

$2/3$ cup chicken stock

salt and pepper

chopped fresh flat-leaf parsley, to garnish

CHICKEN, BEANS, AND SPINACH WITH OLIVES

Heat the oil in a casserole over medium–high heat. Add the chicken and cook until lightly browned all over. Reduce the heat to medium. Add the onion and celery and cook, stirring frequently, for 5 minutes, or until softened.

Stir in the garlic, rosemary, and red pepper flakes and cook, stirring, for 1 minute. Stir in the tomatoes with their juice, beans, and stock. Season with salt and pepper.

Bring to a boil, then reduce the heat and simmer over medium–low heat, stirring occasionally, for 20 minutes. Stir in the spinach leaves and cook for 3 minutes, or until just wilted.

Garnish with the sliced olives and serve immediately.

SERVES 4

2 tbsp olive oil

1 lb 5 oz/600 g skinless, boneless chicken breasts, cut into chunks

1 small onion, finely chopped

2 celery stalks, diced

3 large garlic cloves, finely chopped

2 tsp chopped fresh rosemary

$\frac{1}{4}$ tsp red pepper flakes

14 oz/400 g canned chopped tomatoes in juice

14 oz/400 g canned cannellini beans, drained and rinsed

generous 1 cup chicken stock

$7\frac{1}{2}$ cups baby spinach leaves, coarsely chopped

salt and pepper

8–10 pitted black olives, sliced, to garnish

CHICKEN CASSEROLE

Preheat the oven to 325°F/160°C. Melt the butter with the oil in an ovenproof casserole. Add the chicken pieces and cook until lightly browned all over. Using a slotted spoon, transfer to a plate.

Add the onions and garlic to the casserole and cook over low heat, stirring occasionally, for 10 minutes until golden. Add the tomatoes with their juice, the parsley, basil, tomato paste, and wine and season to taste with salt and pepper. Bring to a boil, then return the chicken pieces to the casserole, pushing them down into the sauce.

Cover the casserole, transfer to the preheated oven, and cook for 50 minutes. Add the mushrooms and cook for an additional 10 minutes, or until the chicken is tender and the juices run clear when a skewer is inserted into the thickest part of the meat. Serve immediately.

SERVES 4

1 tbsp unsalted butter

2 tbsp olive oil

4 lb/1.8 kg skinless chicken portions, on the bone

2 red onions, sliced

2 garlic cloves, finely chopped

14 oz/400 g canned chopped tomatoes in juice

2 tbsp chopped fresh flat-leaf parsley

6 fresh basil leaves, torn

1 tbsp sun-dried tomato paste

$^2/_3$ cup full-bodied red wine

8 oz/225 g mushrooms, sliced

salt and pepper

YOU CAN SUBSTITUTE MARSALA FOR THE RED WINE AND ADD 1 GREEN BELL PEPPER, SEEDED AND SLICED, WITH THE ONIONS AND GARLIC.

DUCKLING WITH LENTILS

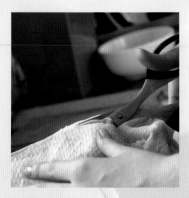

SERVES 4

1 duckling, weighing 5 lb/
2.25 kg

generous 1¹/₈ cups brown lentils

1 tbsp virgin olive oil

2 onions

2 celery stalks

2 tbsp brandy or grappa

²/₃ cup dry white wine

1 tsp cornstarch

salt and pepper

STOCK

wings, backbone, and neck from
the duckling

1 celery stalk

1 garlic clove

6 peppercorns, lightly crushed

1 bay leaf

5 fresh flat-leaf parsley sprigs

1 onion

1 clove

large pinch of salt

Cut the duckling into joints. Cut off the wings. Fold back the skin at the neck end and cut out the wishbone with a small, sharp knife. Using poultry shears or heavy kitchen scissors, cut the breast in half along the breastbone, from the tail end to the neck. Cut along each side of the backbone to separate the 2 halves. Remove the backbone. Cut each portion in half diagonally.

To make the stock, put the wings, backbone, and neck, if available, in a large pan and add the celery, garlic, peppercorns, bay leaf, and parsley. Stick the onion with the clove and add to the pan with the salt. Add cold water to cover and bring to a boil. Skim off any scum that rises to the surface, then reduce the heat and simmer very gently for 2 hours. Strain into a clean pan and boil until reduced and concentrated. Set aside the stock, keeping ²/₃ cup separate from the rest.

Rinse and pick over the lentils, then place in a pan. Add cold water to cover and add the oil. Cut an onion in half and add with a celery stalk. Bring to a boil over medium heat, then reduce the heat and let simmer for 15 minutes, or until the lentils are just beginning to soften. Drain and set aside until required.

Meanwhile, put the duckling pieces, skin-side down, in a heavy-bottomed skillet and cook, gently shaking the skillet occasionally, for 10 minutes. Transfer to an ovenproof casserole and drain off the excess fat from the skillet.

Finely chop the remaining onion and celery and add to the skillet. Cook over a low heat, stirring occasionally, for 5 minutes, or until softened. Using a slotted spoon, transfer the vegetables to the casserole.

Set the casserole over medium heat, add the brandy, and ignite. When the flames have died down, add the wine and the reserved measured stock. Bring to a boil, add the lentils, and season to taste with pepper. Cover and simmer gently over low heat for 40 minutes, until the lentils and duck are tender and the juices run clear when a skewer is inserted into the thickest part of the meat.

Blend the cornstarch with 2 tablespoons of the remaining reserved stock to a smooth paste in a small bowl. Stir the paste into the casserole and cook, stirring constantly, for 5 minutes, or until thickened. Add the salt to taste and adjust the seasoning, if necessary. Serve immediately.

PHEASANT AND CHESTNUT CASSEROLE

Preheat the oven to 350°F/180°C. Melt the oil with the butter in a large skillet over high heat. Add the pheasant joints and cook until browned all over. Using a slotted spoon, transfer the pheasant to a casserole.

Add the bacon to the skillet and cook over medium heat, stirring, for 3–4 minutes until crisp and golden. Transfer to the casserole.

Add the chestnuts to the skillet and cook over low heat, stirring frequently, for 3–4 minutes until lightly browned, then transfer to the casserole.

Add the onions and garlic to the skillet and cook over medium heat, stirring, for 2–3 minutes until the onions are softened.

Stir in the flour and mix well. Gradually add the stock, scraping the sediment from the bottom of the skillet, and bring to a boil. Pour in the wine. Pour over the pheasant in the casserole.

Add the orange rind and juice and the red currant jelly. Season well, cover, and cook in the center of the preheated oven for 1½–2 hours until the pheasant is tender. Turn the joints in the sauce halfway through the cooking time.

Remove from the oven, then check the seasoning and adjust, if necessary.

Serve hot, garnished with the orange slices and watercress.

SERVES 4

1 tbsp olive oil

2 tbsp butter

1 large oven-ready pheasant, jointed

6 oz/175 g lardons or lean bacon, cut into strips

8 oz/225 g vacuum-packed chestnuts

2 onions, thinly sliced

1 garlic clove, chopped

2 tbsp all-purpose flour

scant 2 cups game or vegetable stock

²/₃ cup full-bodied red wine

grated rind and juice of 1 orange

2 tbsp red currant jelly

salt and pepper

TO GARNISH

1 orange, sliced

small bunch of watercress

VENISON CASSEROLE

SERVES 4–6

3 tbsp olive oil

2 lb 4 oz/1 kg casserole venison, cut into 1¼-inch/3-cm cubes

2 onions, thinly sliced

2 garlic cloves, chopped

2 tbsp all-purpose flour

1½ cups beef or vegetable stock

½ cup port or red wine

2 tbsp red currant jelly

6 juniper berries, crushed

pinch of ground cinnamon

freshly grated nutmeg

6 oz/175 g vacuum-packed chestnuts (optional)

salt and pepper

baked or mashed potatoes, to serve

Preheat the oven to 300°F/150°C.

Heat the oil in a large skillet over high heat. Add the venison, in batches if necessary, and cook until browned all over. Using a slotted spoon, transfer to a large casserole.

Add the onions and garlic to the skillet and cook over medium heat, stirring frequently, for 8 minutes, or until golden. Transfer to the casserole. Sprinkle the meat in the casserole with the flour and turn to coat evenly.

Gradually add the stock to the skillet, stirring well and scraping the sediment from the bottom of the skillet, then bring to a boil. Transfer to the casserole and stir well, ensuring that the meat is just covered.

Add the port, red currant jelly, juniper berries, cinnamon, a little freshly grated nutmeg, and the chestnuts, if using. Season well with salt and pepper and stir well. Cover and cook in the center of the preheated oven for 2–2½ hours.

Remove from the oven and adjust the seasoning, if necessary. Serve immediately, piping hot, with baked or mashed potatoes.

THIS CASSEROLE BENEFITS FROM BEING MADE THE DAY BEFORE TO ALLOW THE FLAVORS TO DEVELOP. REHEAT GENTLY BEFORE SERVING. COOL THE CASSEROLE AS QUICKLY AS POSSIBLE AND STORE IN THE REFRIGERATOR OR A COOL PANTRY OVERNIGHT.

RABBIT WITH PRUNES

Put the flour with salt and pepper to taste in a plastic bag, add the rabbit pieces, and shake well to coat each piece.

Melt the butter with the oil in a large sauté pan or skillet with a tight-fitting lid or an ovenproof casserole over medium–high heat. Add the rabbit pieces, in batches if necessary, and cook until lightly browned all over. Using a slotted spoon, transfer to a plate.

Add the shallots, tomato, and garlic to the fat remaining in the pan and cook, stirring frequently, for 3 minutes, or until the shallots are softened but not browned. Return the rabbit pieces to the pan. Add the wine and water to just cover the rabbit—the exact amount will depend on the width of the pan.

Stir in the bouquet garni, cloves, peppercorns, ginger, cinnamon, and salt and pepper to taste. Bring to a boil, stirring, then reduce the heat to low, cover, and let simmer for 45 minutes.

Stir in the prunes and raisins, cover, and simmer for an additional 15 minutes, or until the rabbit pieces are tender when pierced with the tip of a knife. Remove the bouquet garni.

Meanwhile, to make the caramel, put the sugar and water in a small pan over high heat, stirring until the sugar dissolves. Bring to a boil, without stirring, then continue to boil until the syrup turns a dark golden caramel color. Immediately add the vinegar to prevent further cooking.

Stir the caramel into the sauce in the sauté pan. Transfer the rabbit pieces to a serving platter, cover loosely with foil, and keep warm. Bring the sauce to a boil and let bubble and reduce for 2–3 minutes until it has a coating consistency. Taste and adjust the seasoning, if necessary.

Serve the rabbit pieces with the sauce and fruit spooned over, garnished with chopped parsley.

To peel the tomato, use a sharp knife to mark a cross on the base, then place in a heatproof bowl and cover with boiling water. Leave for 5 minutes, rinse under cold water and peel off the skin. Quarter, seed, and chop the flesh.

SERVES 4–6

2 tablespoons all-purpose flour

1 rabbit, weighing 2 lb 12 oz/ 1.25 kg, cut into 8 pieces

2 tbsp unsalted butter

1 tbsp sunflower-seed oil

2 shallots, finely chopped

1 large tomato, peeled, seeded, and diced (see below left)

1 large garlic clove, crushed

generous 1 cup full-bodied red wine

generous 1 cup water

1 bouquet garni

3 cloves

3 black peppercorns, crushed

$^1/_2$ tsp ground ginger

$^1/_4$ tsp ground cinnamon

12–16 no-soak prunes

3 tbsp raisins

salt and pepper

chopped fresh flat-leaf parsley, to garnish

CARAMEL

scant $^1/_4$ cup superfine sugar

2 tbsp water

$^1/_2$ tsp red wine vinegar

PORK CASSEROLE

Spread the flour out on a plate and season to taste with salt and pepper. Toss the pork slices in the flour to coat, shaking off any excess. Heat the oil in an ovenproof casserole over medium heat. Add the pork slices and cook until browned all over. Using a slotted spoon, transfer the pork to a plate.

Add the onions to the casserole and cook over low heat, stirring occasionally, for 10 minutes, or until golden brown. Add the garlic and cook, stirring, for 2 minutes, then add the tomatoes with their juice, the wine, and basil leaves, and season to taste with salt and pepper. Cook, stirring frequently, for 3 minutes.

Return the pork to the casserole, cover, and simmer gently for 1 hour, or until the meat is tender. Stir in the chopped parsley.

Serve immediately, garnished with parsley sprigs, and accompanied by fresh crusty bread.

SERVES 6

scant ⅝ cup all-purpose flour

3 lb/1.3 kg pork tenderloin, cut into ¼-inch/5-mm slices

4 tbsp sunflower-seed oil

2 onions, thinly sliced

2 garlic cloves, finely chopped

14 oz/400 g canned chopped tomatoes in juice

1½ cups dry white wine

1 tbsp torn fresh basil leaves

2 tbsp chopped fresh parsley, plus extra sprigs to garnish

salt and pepper

fresh crusty bread, to serve

BRAISED PORK WITH GARLIC AND HERBS

Preheat the oven to 325°F/160°C. Put the pork, garlic, herbs, peppercorns, pinch of salt, and water to cover in an ovenproof casserole. Cover and bring to a boil, skimming occasionally to remove any scum that rises to the surface. Transfer to the preheated oven and cook, turning the pork occasionally, for 3 hours, or until very tender.

Remove the pork. Strain the stock into a large pitcher. Rinse the casserole, add a ladleful of the stock, and bring to a boil. Add the pork and cook over medium heat until the liquid has almost evaporated.

Continue adding the stock, a ladleful at a time, turning the pork occasionally, until 2 ladlefuls remain.

Transfer the pork to a carving board, cover loosely with foil, and let rest. Add the wine to the casserole, bring to a boil, and cook for 1 minute. Add the remaining stock and boil until reduced by half. Whisk in the butter, a little at a time, then season to taste with salt and pepper.

Carve the pork into thick slices and serve with the sauce, accompanied by green vegetables.

SERVES 6

1 boned and rolled leg of pork, weighing 3 lb 5 oz/1.5 kg

12 garlic cloves, peeled

2 fresh rosemary sprigs

2 fresh sage leaves

4 black peppercorns, lightly crushed

1/2 cup dry white wine

2 tbsp butter, diced

salt and pepper

green vegetables, to serve

SAUSAGES WITH CRANBERRY BEANS

SERVES 4

2 tbsp extra virgin olive oil

1 lb 2 oz/500 g sausages

5 oz/140 g smoked pancetta or lean bacon, diced

2 red onions, chopped

2 garlic cloves, finely chopped

1¹/₃ cups dried cranberry beans, soaked overnight in cold water

2 tsp finely chopped fresh rosemary, plus extra sprigs to garnish

2 tsp chopped fresh sage

1¹/₄ cups dry white wine

1¹/₄ cups water

salt and pepper

fresh crusty bread, to serve

Preheat the oven to 275°F/140°C. Heat the oil in an ovenproof casserole over low heat. Add the sausages and cook until browned all over. Using a slotted spoon, transfer to a plate.

Add the pancetta to the casserole, increase the heat to medium, and cook, stirring frequently, for 5 minutes, or until golden brown. Using a slotted spoon, transfer to the plate.

Add the onions to the casserole and cook over low heat, stirring occasionally, for 5 minutes, or until softened. Add the garlic and cook, stirring, for 2 minutes.

Drain the beans and rinse under cold running water. Put in a large pan of cold water, bring to a boil, and skim off the scum that rises to the surface. Boil rapidly for 10 minutes, then drain.

Add the beans to the casserole, then return the sausages and pancetta. Gently stir in the herbs and pour in the wine and water. Season to taste with pepper. Slowly bring to a boil and boil for 15 minutes, then cover, transfer to the preheated oven, and cook for 2³/₄ hours. Taste and add salt if necessary.

To serve, ladle the sausages and beans onto 4 warmed serving plates. Garnish with rosemary sprigs and serve immediately with fresh crusty bread.

THE BITTER-SWEET FLAVOR OF CRANBERRY BEANS MAKES A PERFECT CONTRAST TO THE SPICINESS OF THE SAUSAGES AND THE SMOKY PANCETTA, BUT OTHER BEANS, SUCH AS CANNELLINI, WOULD WORK WELL TOO.

MARINATED PORK WITH GARLIC

SERVES 6

5 tbsp rice vinegar

4 tbsp dark soy sauce

1 tbsp coriander seeds, crushed

2 lb 4 oz/1 kg boneless pork, cut into 1–1½-inch/2.5–4-cm cubes

1 garlic bulb, separated into cloves and peeled

2 tbsp peanut or sunflower-seed oil

12 oz/350 g sweet potatoes, peeled and cubed

8 black peppercorns, lightly crushed

Mix the vinegar, soy sauce, and crushed coriander seeds together in a shallow, nonmetallic dish. Add the pork cubes and turn to coat in the marinade. Cover and let marinate in the refrigerator for 1 hour.

Slice the garlic cloves lengthwise. Remove the pork from the marinade, setting aside the marinade. Heat the oil in a heavy-bottomed pan over high heat. Add the garlic and cook, stirring, for 1 minute. Reduce the heat to medium, add the pork, and cook, stirring, for 5 minutes. Add the sweet potatoes, peppercorns, the reserved marinade, and water to cover. Bring to a boil, skim off any scum that rises to the surface, then reduce the heat, cover, and simmer for 30 minutes.

Uncover the pan, increase the heat to high, and cook, stirring frequently, for 25 minutes, or until the pork is tender and the sauce is slightly thickened. Serve hot.

LAMB TAGINE

SERVES 4

1 tbsp sunflower-seed or corn oil

1 onion, chopped

12 oz/350 g boneless lamb, trimmed of all visible fat and cut into 1-inch/2.5-cm cubes

1 garlic clove, finely chopped

2¹/₂ cups vegetable stock

grated rind and juice of 1 orange

1 tsp honey

1 cinnamon stick

¹/₂-inch/1-cm piece fresh gingerroot, finely chopped

1 eggplant

4 tomatoes, peeled and chopped

²/₃ cup no-soak dried apricots

2 tbsp chopped fresh cilantro

salt and pepper

freshly cooked couscous, to serve

Heat the oil in a large, heavy-bottomed skillet with a tight-fitting lid or ovenproof casserole over medium heat. Add the onion and lamb cubes and cook until the meat is lightly browned all over. Add the garlic, stock, orange rind and juice, honey, cinnamon stick, and ginger. Bring to a boil, then reduce the heat, cover, and let simmer for 45 minutes.

Halve the eggplant lengthwise and slice thinly. Add to the skillet with the tomatoes and apricots. Cover and cook for an additional 45 minutes, until the lamb is tender.

Stir in the cilantro, season to taste with salt and pepper, and serve immediately, straight from the skillet, with couscous.

BRAISED LAMB SHANKS WITH CANNELLINI BEANS

Preheat the oven to 325°F/160°C. Drain the beans and rinse under cold running water. Put in a large pan of cold water, bring to a boil, and skim off the scum that rises to the surface. Boil rapidly for 10 minutes, then drain and set aside.

Meanwhile, heat the oil in a large, ovenproof casserole over medium heat. Add the onion and cook, stirring frequently, for 5 minutes, or until softened. Add the carrots and celery and cook, stirring frequently, for 5 minutes, or until beginning to soften and the onion is beginning to brown. Add the garlic and cook, stirring, for 1 minute. Push the vegetables to one side.

Add the lamb shanks to the casserole and cook until browned all over. Add the reserved beans, tomatoes with their juice, the wine, and orange rind and juice and stir together. Add the bay leaves and rosemary. Pour in the water so that the liquid comes halfway up the shanks. Season with pepper, but do not add salt as this will prevent the beans softening.

Bring to a boil, then cover, transfer to the preheated oven, and cook for 1 hour. Turn the shanks over in the stock and cook for an additional 1¹⁄₂ hours until the lamb and beans are tender. Remove the bay leaves, then taste and add salt and pepper, if necessary. Serve hot.

SERVES 4

1¹⁄₂ cups dried cannellini beans, soaked overnight in cold water

2 tbsp sunflower-seed or corn oil

1 large onion, thinly sliced

4 carrots, chopped

2 celery stalks, thinly sliced

1 garlic clove, chopped

4 large lamb shanks

14 oz/400 g canned chopped tomatoes in juice

1¹⁄₄ cups full-bodied red wine

thinly pared rind and juice of 1 orange

2 bay leaves

3 fresh rosemary sprigs

scant 1 cup water

salt and pepper

VEAL WITH GREMOLATA

Melt the butter with the oil in a large, heavy-bottomed skillet over low heat. Add the onions and leek and cook, stirring occasionally, for 5 minutes, or until softened.

Spread the flour out on a plate and season to taste with salt and pepper. Toss the pieces of veal in the flour to coat, shaking off any excess. Add the veal to the skillet, increase the heat to high, and cook until browned all over.

Gradually stir in the wine and stock and bring just to a boil, stirring constantly. Reduce the heat, cover, and simmer for 1¼ hours, or until the veal is very tender.

Meanwhile, to make the gremolata, mix all the ingredients together in a small bowl.

Using a slotted spoon, transfer the veal to a warmed serving dish, and keep warm. Bring the sauce to a boil and cook, stirring occasionally, until thickened and reduced.

Pour the sauce over the veal, sprinkle with the gremolata, and serve immediately.

SERVES 4

4 tbsp butter

1 tbsp extra virgin olive oil

2 onions, chopped

1 leek, chopped

3 tbsp all-purpose flour

4 thick slices veal shin

1¼ cups dry white wine

1¼ cups veal or chicken stock

salt and pepper

GREMOLATA

2 tbsp finely chopped fresh parsley

1 garlic clove, very finely chopped

grated rind of 1 lemon

MODERN VERSIONS OF THIS DISH OFTEN INCLUDE TOMATOES. IF YOU LIKE, ADD 14 OZ/400 G CANNED TOMATOES WITH THE WINE AND STOCK. YOU COULD ALSO ADD 1 FINELY CHOPPED CARROT AND 1 FINELY CHOPPED CELERY STALK WITH THE ONIONS AND LEEK.

BEEF CASSEROLE

Preheat the oven to 300°F/150°C. Melt 2 tablespoons of the butter with 1 tablespoon of the oil in a large, ovenproof casserole over medium–high heat. Add the lardons and cook for 2 minutes, or until beginning to brown. Remove with a slotted spoon and drain on paper towels.

Add the beef, in batches if necessary, and cook until browned all over. Add extra butter or oil as necessary. Transfer to a plate.

Pour off all but 2 tablespoons of the fat from the casserole. Add the garlic, carrot, leek, and onion and cook, stirring frequently, for 3 minutes, or until the onion is beginning to soften. Sprinkle in the flour with salt and pepper to taste and cook, stirring, for 2 minutes.

Stir in the wine, stock, tomato paste, and the bouquet garni and bring to a boil, scraping the sediment from the bottom of the casserole. Return the beef and lardons to the casserole and pour in extra stock so that the ingredients are covered by about 1/2 inch/1 cm.

Slowly return the casserole to a boil, then cover, transfer to the preheated oven, and cook for 2 hours.

Meanwhile, melt 2 tablespoons of the remaining butter with the remaining oil in a large sauté pan or skillet over medium–high heat. Add the pickling onions and cook, stirring frequently, until golden all over. Remove with a slotted spoon and set aside.

Melt the remaining butter in the sauté pan. Add the mushrooms, season to taste with salt and pepper, and cook, stirring, until golden. Remove with a slotted spoon and set aside.

After the casserole has cooked for 2 hours, stir in the pickling onions and mushrooms. Cook for an additional 30 minutes, or until the beef is very tender.

Remove the bouquet garni. Taste and adjust the seasoning, if necessary. Sprinkle over the parsley to garnish and serve hot with French bread.

SERVES 4–6

6 tbsp butter

2 tbsp sunflower-seed oil

6 oz/175 g smoked lardons, blanched for 30 seconds, drained, and patted dry

2 lb/900 g stewing beef, such as chuck or leg, trimmed and cut into 2-inch/5-cm chunks

2 large garlic cloves, crushed

1 carrot, peeled and diced

1 leek, halved and sliced

1 onion, finely chopped

2 tbsp all-purpose flour

1½ cups full-bodied red wine

generous 2 cups beef stock

1 tbsp tomato paste

1 bouquet garni

12 pickling onions

12 white mushrooms

salt and pepper

chopped fresh flat-leaf parsley, to garnish

French bread, to serve

LONE STAR CHILI

Dry-fry the cumin seeds in a heavy-bottomed skillet over medium heat, shaking the pan frequently, for 3–4 minutes until lightly toasted. Let cool, then crush in a mortar with a pestle.

Put the flour in a bowl and season to taste with salt and pepper. Toss the beef in the flour to coat, shaking off any excess. Melt the drippings in a large, heavy-bottomed pan. Add the beef, in batches, and cook until browned all over. Using a slotted spoon, transfer the beef to a plate.

Add the onions and garlic to the pan and cook over medium heat, stirring, for 5 minutes, or until the onions are softened. Add the cumin, oregano, paprika, and chiles and cook, stirring, for 2 minutes. Return the beef to the pan, pour over the lager, then add the chocolate. Bring to a boil, stirring, then reduce the heat, cover, and let simmer for 2–3 hours until the beef is very tender, adding more lager if necessary. Serve with warmed flour tortillas and some sour cream.

SERVES 4

1 tbsp cumin seeds

all-purpose flour

1 lb 7 oz/650 g rump steak, cut into 1-inch/2.5-cm cubes

3 tbsp beef drippings, bacon fat, or vegetable oil

2 onions, finely chopped

4 garlic cloves, finely chopped

1 tbsp dried oregano

2 tsp paprika

4 red pepper flakes, crushed, or to taste

1 large bottle of Spanish lager

4 oz/115 g semisweet chocolate

salt and pepper

TO SERVE

warmed flour tortillas

sour cream

BEEF STEW WITH GARLIC AND SHALLOTS

Spread the flour out on a plate and season to taste with salt and pepper. Toss the steak in the flour to coat. Heat 3 tablespoons of the oil in a large, ovenproof casserole. Add the steak, in batches, and cook until browned all over. Using a slotted spoon, transfer to a plate.

Heat the remaining oil in the casserole over medium heat. Add the garlic and cook, stirring frequently, until golden. Add the vinegar and heat until evaporated. Transfer the garlic to the plate.

Melt the butter in the casserole over low heat. Add the shallots and cook, stirring frequently, for 15 minutes. Remove and set aside.

Return the steak and garlic to the casserole. Add the wine and salt and pepper to taste. Bring to a boil, stirring. Reduce the heat, cover, and simmer, stirring occasionally, for 1–1$\frac{1}{4}$ hours. Return the shallots to the casserole, cover, and cook for an additional 45 minutes, or until the beef is tender. Garnish with thyme sprigs and serve.

SERVES 6

4 tbsp all-purpose flour

3 lb/1.3 kg top round steak, cut into 2-inch/5-cm cubes

4 tbsp sunflower-seed oil

12 garlic cloves, lightly crushed

3 tbsp sherry vinegar

4 tbsp butter

1 lb 14 oz/850 g shallots

1$\frac{1}{2}$ cups full-bodied red wine

salt and pepper

few fresh thyme sprigs, to garnish

BEEF STEW WITH OLIVES

SERVES 4–6

2 lb/900 g stewing beef, such as chuck or leg, trimmed and cut into 2-inch/5-cm cubes

2 onions, thinly sliced

2 carrots, thickly sliced

4 large garlic cloves, bruised

1 large bouquet garni of 2 fresh flat-leaf parsley sprigs, 2 fresh thyme sprigs, and 2 bay leaves, tied to a piece of celery

4 juniper berries

generous 2 cups full-bodied red wine

2 tbsp brandy

2 tbsp olive oil

8 oz/225 g boned belly of pork (side pork), rind removed

scant $1\frac{3}{8}$ cups all-purpose flour

2 x 4-inch/10-cm strips of orange rind

$\frac{1}{2}$ cup black olives, pitted and rinsed

beef stock, if necessary

$\frac{1}{3}$ cup water

salt and pepper

pasta, to serve

TO GARNISH

chopped fresh flat-leaf parsley

finely grated orange rind

Put the beef in a large glass or earthenware bowl and add the onions, carrots, garlic, bouquet garni, juniper berries, and salt and pepper to taste. Pour over the wine, brandy, and oil and stir well. Cover and let marinate in the refrigerator for 24 hours.

Remove the beef and marinade from the refrigerator 30 minutes before cooking. Preheat the oven to 325°F/160°C. Cut the pork into $\frac{1}{4}$-inch/5-mm strips. Bring a pan of water to a boil and add the pork. Return to a boil and blanch for 3 minutes, then drain.

Remove the beef from the marinade, setting aside the marinade, and pat dry with paper towels. Put 3 tablespoons of the flour with salt and pepper to taste in a plastic bag, add the beef, and shake well to coat each piece.

Transfer half the pork strips to a 3.5-quart ovenproof casserole. Top with the beef and marinade, including the vegetables and bouquet garni, and add the orange rind and olives. Scatter the remaining pork strips over. If the wine doesn't cover all the ingredients, top off with stock.

Mix the remaining flour with the water in a small bowl to form a

thick, pliable paste. Slowly bring the casserole to a boil, then add the lid and use your fingers to press the paste around the rim to form a tight seal. Transfer the casserole to the preheated oven and cook for 1 hour. Reduce the temperature to 275°F/140°C and cook for an additional 3 hours.

Remove the casserole from the oven and use a serrated knife to cut off the seal. Use the tip of the knife to ensure that the beef and carrots are tender. If not, cook for an additional 15 minutes.

Using a large metal spoon, skim any fat from the surface. Season to taste. Remove the bouquet garni, sprinkle the parsley and orange rind over the top, and serve with pasta. Alternatively, let cool completely, cover, and let chill overnight. Before reheating, scrape the solid fat off the surface.

7

PIES AND PASTRIES

If you're looking for an alternative to sandwiches, check out
the following pages for fresh ideas. Portable picnic foods
abound in this chapter, with recipes for tartlets of numerous
varieties, from Balsamic Duck and Radicchio to Artichoke and
Pancetta. Find out how to make a delicious Pork and Apple Pie
or Rosemary Lamb in Phyllo Pastry. There are plenty of supper
standbys as well, from traditional Potato-Topped Lamb Pie
to Beef in Puff Pastry and Steak and Mushroom Pie.

BALSAMIC DUCK AND RADICCHIO TARTLETS

Grease a 3-inch/7.5-cm, 12-hole muffin pan. To make the pie dough, sift the flour and salt into a food processor, add the butter, and process until the mixture resembles fine bread crumbs. Tip into a large bowl. Alternatively, sift the flour and salt into a bowl and rub in the butter with your fingertips until the mixture resembles fine bread crumbs. Stir in the sugar and mix in a little iced water, just enough to bring the dough together.

Turn out onto a lightly floured counter and cut the dough in half. Roll out one half and, using a 3¹/₂-inch/9-cm pastry cutter, cut out 6 circles. Roll out each circle to 4¹/₂ inches/12 cm in diameter and use to line the muffin holes, pressing to fit. Repeat with the remaining dough. Put a piece of parchment paper in each hole and fill with dried beans. Let chill for 30 minutes. Meanwhile, preheat the oven to 400°F/200°C.

Bake the tartlet shells in the preheated oven for 10 minutes, then remove the paper and beans and bake for an additional 5 minutes. Let cool in the pan until cold. Leave the oven on.

To make the filling, wipe the duck breasts with paper towels, make a series of thin, diagonal cuts in the skin, and rub in the salt. Put the duck on a rack set over a roasting pan. Roast for 25–30 minutes until crisp. Meanwhile, melt the butter with the oil in a skillet over low heat. Add the onions and sugar and cook, stirring occasionally, for 20–25 minutes, until soft and slightly caramelized. Add the vinegar, radicchio, and salt and pepper to taste and cook, stirring frequently, for an additional 5 minutes. Remove the duck from the oven and let rest for 5 minutes.

Put the tartlet shells on a serving dish and spoon in the onion and radicchio mixture. Slice the duck very thinly and divide between the tarts. Sprinkle with parsley and drizzle with a little more balsamic vinegar. Serve warm.

MAKES 12

PIE DOUGH

7 tbsp butter, diced and chilled, plus extra for greasing

scant 1⁵/₈ cups all-purpose flour, plus extra for dusting

pinch of salt

¹/₂ tsp confectioners' sugar

1–2 tbsp iced water

FILLING

2 duck breasts, about 6 oz/175 g each

pinch of salt

2 tbsp butter

1 tbsp olive oil

2 onions, thinly sliced

2 tsp brown sugar

1 tbsp balsamic vinegar, plus extra for drizzling

¹/₂ large or 1 small radicchio, thinly shredded

salt and pepper

chopped fresh flat-leaf parsley, to garnish

READY-COOKED CHINESE DUCK WOULD ALSO WORK WELL IF REHEATED AND SHREDDED. SUBSTITUTE SOY SAUCE FOR THE BALSAMIC VINEGAR AND SIMMER UNTIL THICK, THEN DRIZZLE OVER THE DUCK AND TOP WITH SHREDDED SCALLION. THINLY PARED STRIPS OF ORANGE RIND WOULD ALSO MAKE AN ATTRACTIVE GARNISH.

QUICHE LORRAINE TARTLETS

MAKES 6

PIE DOUGH

scant 1¼ cups all-purpose flour

pinch of salt

6 tbsp chilled unsalted butter, diced

2–3 tbsp iced water

FILLING

4½ oz/125 g unsmoked lardons

2 large eggs

1 cup whipping cream

4½ oz/125 g Gruyère cheese, grated

freshly grated nutmeg

salt and pepper

Grease 6 x 4½-inch/12-cm tart pans. To make the pie dough, sift the flour and salt into a food processor, add the butter, and process until the mixture resembles fine bread crumbs. Alternatively, sift the flour and salt into a bowl and rub in the butter with your fingertips until the mixture resembles fine bread crumbs. Tip into a large bowl, if necessary, and mix in about 2 tablespoons of iced water, just enough to bring the dough together. Lightly sprinkle with extra water.

Turn out onto a lightly floured counter and cut into 6 equal-size pieces. Roll out each piece and use to line each tart pan,

pressing to fit. Leave the excess dough hanging over the edges of the rims. Put a piece of parchment paper into each tartlet and fill with dried beans. Let chill for 30 minutes. Meanwhile, preheat the oven to 400°F/200°C.

Bake the tartlet shells in the preheated oven for 5 minutes, or until the rim is set. Remove the paper and beans, then return the tart shells to the oven and bake for an additional 5 minutes, or until the bases look dry. Leave the tart shells on the cookie sheet and remove from the oven. Reduce the oven temperature to 375°F/190°C.

Meanwhile, put the lardons in a sauté pan or skillet over low heat and sauté for 3 minutes, or until the fat begins to melt. Increase the heat to medium and continue sautéeing until they are crisp.

Sprinkle the lardons over the pastry shell. Beat the eggs, cream, and cheese together, then season to taste with the salt and pepper and nutmeg. Carefully divide the filling between the pastry shells, then transfer the tarts to the oven to bake for 20–25 minutes until the filling is set and the pastry is golden brown. Transfer the quiches to a cooling rack to cool completely, then remove from the pans.

PEA, HAM, AND SOUR CREAM TARTLETS

MAKES 6

PIE DOUGH

5 tbsp butter, diced and chilled, plus extra for greasing

scant 1 cup all-purpose flour, plus extra for dusting

pinch of salt

$^1/_4$ cup freshly grated Parmesan cheese

1–2 tbsp iced water

FILLING

1$^3/_4$ cups fresh or frozen peas

2 tbsp unsalted butter

2 shallots, finely chopped

3$^1/_2$ oz/100 g cooked ham, chopped

3–4 fresh mint leaves, chopped

$^1/_2$ cup sour cream

3 egg yolks

salt and pepper

Grease 6 x 3$^1/_2$-inch/9-cm loose-bottomed fluted tart pans. To make the pie dough, sift the flour and salt into a food processor, add the butter, and process until the mixture resembles fine bread crumbs. Alternatively, sift the flour and salt into a bowl and rub in the butter with your fingertips until the mixture resembles fine bread crumbs. Stir in the Parmesan cheese and mix in a little iced water, just enough to bring the dough together.

Turn out onto a lightly floured counter and cut into 6 equal-size pieces. Roll out each piece and use to line each tart pan, pressing to fit. Roll the rolling pin over the pans to neaten the edges and trim the excess dough. Put a piece of parchment paper into each tartlet and fill with dried beans. Let chill for 30 minutes. Meanwhile, preheat the oven to 400°F/200°C.

Bake the tartlet shells in the preheated oven for 10 minutes, then remove the paper and beans.

Meanwhile, to make the filling, cook the peas in a pan of boiling water for 3–4 minutes until just tender, then drain. Melt the butter in a skillet over low heat. Add the shallots and cook, stirring occasionally, for 10 minutes. Add the ham and cook, stirring, for 3–5 minutes. Add the peas and mint, remove from the heat, and stir in the sour cream and egg yolks. Season with salt and pepper. Divide between the tartlet shells. Bake for 12–15 minutes. Serve warm.

ARTICHOKE AND PANCETTA TARTLETS

MAKES 6

PIE DOUGH

5 tbsp butter, diced and chilled, plus extra for greasing

scant 1 cup all-purpose flour, plus extra for dusting

pinch of salt

1–2 tbsp iced water

FILLING

5 tbsp heavy cream

4 tbsp bottled artichoke paste, tapenade, or pesto

14 oz/400 g canned artichoke hearts, drained

12 thin-cut pancetta strips

salt and pepper

TO SERVE

arugula leaves

1³/₄ oz/50 g Parmesan or romano cheese

2 tbsp olive oil, for drizzling

Grease 6 x 3¹/₂-inch/9-cm loose-bottomed fluted tart pans. To make the pie dough, sift the flour and salt into a food processor, add the butter, and process until the mixture resembles fine bread crumbs. Tip into a large bowl. Alternatively, sift the flour and salt into a bowl and rub in the butter with your fingertips until the mixture resembles fine bread crumbs. Mix in just enough iced water to bring the dough together.

Turn out onto a lightly floured counter and cut into 6 equal-size pieces. Roll out each piece and use to line each tart pan, pressing to fit. Roll the rolling pin over the pans to neaten the edges and trim the excess dough. Put a piece of parchment paper into each tartlet and fill with dried beans. Let chill for 30 minutes. Meanwhile, preheat the oven to 400°F/200°C.

Bake the tartlet shells in the preheated oven for 10 minutes, then remove the paper and beans.

Meanwhile, to make the filling, stir the cream and artichoke paste together in a bowl and season well with salt and pepper. Divide between the tartlet shells, spreading out to cover the base of each tartlet. Cut each artichoke heart into 3 pieces and divide between the tartlets. Curl 2 strips of the pancetta into each tart. Bake for 10 minutes.

To serve, top each tartlet with a few arugula leaves. Using a potato peeler, shave the Parmesan cheese and scatter the shavings over the tartlets. Drizzle with oil and serve.

PHYLLO CHICKEN PIE

Put the chicken in a large pan and add the onion halves, carrot, celery, bay leaf, lemon rind, and peppercorns. Pour in enough cold water to just cover the chicken legs and bring to a boil. Reduce the heat, cover, and simmer for 1 hour, or until tender and the juices run clear when a skewer is inserted into the thickest part of the meat. Remove the chicken from the pan and let cool.

Bring the stock to a boil and boil until reduced to 2¹/₂ cups. Strain and set aside the stock.

When the chicken is cool enough to handle, remove the flesh, discarding the skin and bones. Cut the flesh into bite-size pieces.

To make the filling, melt 4 tablespoons of the butter in a pan over medium heat. Add the chopped onions and cook, stirring frequently, for 5 minutes, or until softened. Stir in the flour and cook over low heat, stirring, for 1–2 minutes. Remove from the heat and gradually stir in the reserved stock and the milk. Return to the heat and bring to a boil, stirring constantly, then reduce the heat and let simmer for 1–2 minutes until thickened and smooth.

Remove from the heat, stir in the chicken, and season to taste with salt and pepper. Let cool. Meanwhile, preheat the oven to 375°F/190°C.

When the chicken mixture has cooled, stir in the cheese and eggs and mix together well.

Melt the remaining butter in a pan and use a little to lightly grease a deep 12 x 8-inch/30 x 20-cm roasting pan.

Cut the pastry sheets in half widthwise. Take one sheet of pastry and cover the remaining sheets with a damp dish towel. Use the sheet to line the pan and brush with a little of the melted butter. Repeat with half the pastry sheets, brushing each with butter.

Spread the chicken filling over the pastry, then top with the remaining pastry sheets, brushing each with butter and tucking down the edges. Using a sharp knife, score the top layers of the pastry into 6 squares.

Bake the pie in a preheated oven for 50 minutes, or until golden brown. Remove from the oven and let rest in a warm place for 5–10 minutes, then serve hot, cut into squares.

SERVES 6–8

1 chicken, weighing 3 lb 5 oz/ 1.5 kg

1 small onion, halved, and 3 large onions, finely chopped

1 carrot, thickly sliced

1 celery stalk, thickly sliced

1 bay leaf

thinly pared rind of 1 lemon

10 peppercorns

11 tbsp butter

generous ³/₈ cup all-purpose flour

²/₃ cup milk

1 oz/25 g romano cheese, grated

3 eggs, beaten

8 oz/225 g ready-made phyllo pastry, thawed if frozen

salt and pepper

TURKEY PIE

To make the pie dough, sift the flour and salt into a bowl. Rub in the margarine and shortening with your fingertips until the mixture resembles fine bread crumbs. Mix in just enough iced water to bring the dough together. Wrap in plastic wrap and let chill for 30 minutes.

Preheat the oven to 375°F/190°C. Melt half the butter in a pan over medium heat, stir in the flour, and cook, stirring constantly, for 1 minute. Gradually whisk in the stock and bring to a boil, whisking constantly. Reduce the heat and simmer for 2 minutes, then stir in the cream. Season to taste with salt and pepper.

Melt the remaining butter in a large skillet over low heat. Add the onion and carrots and cook, stirring occasionally, for 5 minutes, or until softened. Add the celery and mushrooms and cook, stirring occasionally, for 5 minutes, then stir in the turkey and peas. Stir into the cream sauce, then transfer to a large pie dish.

Roll out the pie dough on a lightly floured counter to about $1/8$ inch/3 mm thick. Cut out a rectangle about 1 inch/2.5 cm larger than the dish and lay it over the filling. Crimp the edges, cut 3–4 slits in the top to allow the steam to escape and brush with the beaten egg to glaze. Roll out the trimmings and cut out shapes to decorate the pie, if you like.

Bake the pie in the preheated oven for 30 minutes until golden brown. Serve immediately.

SERVES 6

4 tbsp butter

2 tbsp all-purpose flour

1 cup chicken stock

3 tbsp heavy cream

1 onion, chopped

2 carrots, sliced

2 celery stalks, chopped

2 oz/55 g mushrooms, sliced

1 lb/450 g cooked turkey, diced

$1/2$ cup frozen peas

1 egg, lightly beaten

salt and pepper

PIE DOUGH

scant $1^5/8$ cups all-purpose flour, plus extra for dusting

pinch of salt

8 tbsp margarine, diced and chilled

4 tbsp shortening or white vegetable fat, diced and chilled

1–2 tbsp iced water

GAME PIE

Preheat the oven to 325°F/160°C. Oil a 1-quart pie dish. Put the flour with salt and pepper to taste in a large plastic bag, add the meat, and shake well to coat each piece.

Heat the oil in a large casserole over high heat. Add the meat, in batches, and cook until browned all over. Remove with a slotted spoon and keep warm. Add the onion and garlic and cook, stirring, for 2–3 minutes until softened, then add the mushrooms and cook for 2 minutes, stirring constantly, until beginning to wilt. Add the juniper berries, then the port and scrape the sediment from the bottom of the casserole. Add the stock and bring to a boil, stirring constantly. Let bubble for 2–3 minutes. Add the bay leaf and return the meat to the casserole.

Cover, transfer to the preheated oven, and cook for 1¹/₂–2 hours until the meat is tender. Taste and adjust the seasoning, if necessary. Let cool,

then let chill overnight to develop the flavors. Remove the bay leaf.

Preheat the oven to 400°F/200°C. Roll out the ready-made puff pastry on a lightly floured counter to about 2³/₄ inches/7 cm larger than the pie dish. Cut off a 1¹/₄-inch/3-cm strip around the edge. Moisten the rim of the dish and press the pastry strip onto it. Put a pie funnel in the center of the dish and spoon in the meat filling. Don't overfill—and keep any extra gravy to serve separately.

Moisten the pastry collar with a little water and put on the pastry lid. Crimp the edges of the pastry firmly and brush with the beaten egg to glaze.

Bake the pie on a cookie sheet near the top of the preheated oven for 30 minutes, or until golden brown and the filling is bubbling hot. Cover with foil and reduce the oven temperature a little if the pastry is getting too brown.

SERVES 4–6

3 tbsp vegetable oil, plus extra for oiling

2 tbsp all-purpose flour, plus extra for dusting

1 lb 9 oz/700 g mixed game, cut into 1¹/₄-inch/3-cm pieces

1 onion, coarsely chopped

1 garlic clove, finely chopped

12 oz/350 g large portobello mushrooms, sliced

1 tsp crushed juniper berries

¹/₂ cup port or Marsala

2 cups chicken or game stock

1 bay leaf

14 oz/400 g ready-made puff pastry, thawed if frozen

1 egg, beaten

salt and pepper

RABBIT, ROAST TOMATO, AND SAGE PIE

SERVES 4

1 lb/450 g cherry tomatoes

3 tbsp olive oil

¹/₂ tsp sugar

1 tbsp all-purpose flour

1 lb 9 oz/700 g boned rabbit, cubed

1 onion, chopped

1 garlic clove, finely chopped

generous ¹/₈ cup pine nuts

²/₃ cup chicken or vegetable stock

1 tbsp lemon juice

12 fresh sage leaves, finely chopped

2¹/₂ tbsp butter

3¹/₂ oz/100 g ready-made phyllo pastry, thawed if frozen

salt and pepper

Preheat the oven to 400°F/200°C. Put the tomatoes in a roasting pan and sprinkle with 1 tablespoon of the oil and the sugar. Roast in the preheated oven for 30 minutes.

Meanwhile, put the flour in a plastic bag, add the rabbit, and shake well to coat each piece. Heat 1 tablespoon of the remaining oil in a large, heavy-bottom skillet over medium heat. Add the onion and garlic and cook, stirring frequently, for 5 minutes, or until softened. Add the pine nuts and cook, stirring, for 1 minute. Using a slotted spoon, transfer the mixture to a 1¹/₂-quart pie dish.

Heat the remaining oil in the skillet over medium–high heat. Add the rabbit and cook until browned all over. Add the stock and lemon juice and bring to a boil, stirring constantly. Reduce the heat and simmer for 2–3 minutes. Transfer the mixture to the pie dish.

When the tomatoes have roasted, gently stir them into the pie dish. Add the sage and season to taste with salt and pepper.

Reduce the oven temperature to 375°F/190°C. Melt the butter in a pan over low heat. Take one sheet of pastry and cover the remaining sheets with a damp dish towel. Brush the sheet with a little of the melted butter, then cut into 1-inch/2.5-cm strips. Arrange on top of the pie. Repeat with the remaining pastry sheets, brushing each with butter and arranging on top of the pie in the opposite direction each time. Make sure that the filling is covered and tuck in the edges.

Bake the pie in the oven for 30 minutes, or until golden brown. Serve hot.

PORK AND APPLE PIE

To make the filling, cook the potatoes in a pan of boiling water for 10 minutes. Drain and set aside. Melt the butter with the oil in an ovenproof casserole over medium–high heat. Add the pork and cook until browned all over. Add the onion and garlic and cook, stirring frequently, for 5 minutes. Stir in the remaining filling ingredients, except the potatoes and apples. Season to taste with salt and pepper. Reduce the heat,

cover, and simmer for $1^1/2$ hours. Drain the stock from the casserole and set aside. Let the pork cool.

Preheat the oven to 400°F/200°C. To make the pie dough, sift the flour and salt into a bowl. Make a well in the center. Melt the butter and shortening in a pan with the water, then bring to a boil. Pour into the well and gradually mix into the flour to form a dough. Turn out onto a lightly floured counter and knead until smooth. Set aside a quarter of the dough and use the remainder to line the base and side of a large pie pan or deep 8-inch/20-cm round loose-bottom cake pan.

Layer the pork, potatoes, and apples in the base. Roll out the reserved dough to make a lid. Dampen the edges and put the lid on top, sealing well. Brush with the beaten egg to glaze. Make a hole in the top. Bake in the preheated oven for 30 minutes, then reduce the temperature to 325°F/160°C and bake for an additional 45 minutes. Dissolve the gelatin in the reserved stock and pour into the hole in the lid as the pie cools. Serve well chilled.

SERVES 8

FILLING

2 lb/900 g waxy potatoes, sliced

2 tbsp butter

2 tbsp vegetable oil

1 lb/450 g lean boneless pork, cubed

2 onions, sliced

4 garlic cloves, crushed

4 tbsp tomato paste

$2^1/2$ cups stock

2 tbsp chopped fresh sage

2 eating apples, peeled, cored, and sliced

salt and pepper

PIE DOUGH

1 lb 8 oz/675 g all-purpose flour, plus extra for dusting

pinch of salt

4 tbsp butter

9 tbsp shortening

$1^1/4$ cups water

1 egg, beaten

1 tsp gelatin

POTATO AND HAM PIE

SERVES 12

8 oz/225 g waxy potatoes, cubed

2 tbsp butter

8 shallots, halved

8 oz/225 g smoked ham, cubed

2^1/$_2$ tbsp all-purpose flour

1^1/$_4$ cups milk

2 tbsp whole grain mustard

1^3/$_4$ oz/50 g pineapple, cubed

salt and pepper

PIE DOUGH

scant 1^5/$_8$ cups all-purpose flour, plus extra for dusting

^{1}/$_2$ tsp mustard powder

pinch of salt

pinch of cayenne pepper

11 tbsp butter, diced and chilled

4^1/$_2$ oz/125 g sharp Cheddar cheese, grated

2 egg yolks, plus extra for glazing

4–6 tsp iced water

Cook the potato cubes in a pan of boiling water for 10 minutes. Drain and set aside.

Meanwhile, melt the butter in a separate pan over low heat. Add the shallots and cook, stirring frequently, for 3–4 minutes until beginning to brown.

Add the ham and cook, stirring, for 2–3 minutes. Stir in the flour and cook, stirring, for 1 minute. Gradually stir in the milk. Add the mustard and pineapple and bring to a boil, stirring. Season well with salt and pepper and add the potato.

Preheat the oven to 375°F/190°C. To make the pie dough, sift the flour, mustard powder, salt, and cayenne pepper into a bowl. Rub in the butter with your fingertips until the mixture resembles fine

bread crumbs. Stir in the cheese. Add the egg yolks and water and mix to form a dough. Turn out onto a lightly floured counter. Cut the pie dough in half. Roll out one half and use to line a shallow pie dish.

Spoon the filling into the pie dish. Brush the edges with water. Roll out the remaining dough and press it on top of the pie, sealing the edges. Decorate with the trimmings. Brush with egg yolk to glaze and bake in the preheated oven for 40–45 minutes, or until golden brown.

ROSEMARY LAMB IN PHYLLO PASTRY

Heat 2 tablespoons of the oil in a heavy-bottom pan over medium heat. Add the onion and garlic and cook, stirring frequently, for 5 minutes, or until the onion is softened. Add the spinach and nutmeg and cook, stirring, for 3 minutes.

Turn into a food processor or blender, add the yogurt, and salt and pepper to taste, and process until smooth. Let the mixture cool.

Meanwhile, heat the remaining oil in a skillet over medium–high heat. Add the lamb fillets and rosemary and cook for 3 minutes on each side. Remove from the skillet, drain on paper towels and let cool.

Preheat the oven to 375°F/190°C. When the lamb fillets are cool, slash each fillet 4 times, almost all the way through. Fill each slash with the spinach mixture, spreading any remaining mixture on top. Season the fillets to taste with salt and pepper.

Melt the butter in a pan over low heat. Take one sheet of pastry and cover the remaining sheets with a damp dish towel. Brush the sheet with a little of the melted butter. Put a second sheet on top, brush with butter and fold both sheets in half. Put a lamb fillet in the center and wrap to form a package. Put on a cookie sheet and brush with butter. Repeat with the remaining pastry and lamb fillets to form 4 packages.

Bake the lamb packages in the preheated oven for 25 minutes until golden. Serve hot.

SERVES 4

3 tbsp olive oil

1 small onion, finely chopped

1 garlic clove, finely chopped

3³/₄ cups spinach leaves

pinch of freshly grated nutmeg

2 tbsp strained plain yogurt

4 lamb loin fillets, about 4 oz/115 g each

1 tsp finely chopped fresh rosemary leaves

5 tbsp butter

8 sheets ready-made phyllo pastry, thawed if frozen

salt and pepper

PORK FILLET (TENDERLOIN) CAN BE USED IN EXACTLY THE SAME WAY AS THE LAMB AND, INSTEAD OF THE SPINACH PURÉE, YOU COULD USE A LEEK PURÉE WITH EITHER MEAT. PREPARE THIS IN THE SAME WAY AS THE SPINACH PURÉE IN THE RECIPE, BUT SUBSTITUTE THE SPINACH LEAVES WITH THE SAME QUANTITY OF SLICED LEEKS AND COOK FOR 10 MINUTES UNTIL TENDER.

POTATO-TOPPED LAMB PIE

SERVES 6

1 tbsp olive oil

2 onions, finely chopped

2 garlic cloves, finely chopped

1 lb 8 oz/675 g good-quality
fresh ground lamb

2 carrots, finely chopped

1 tbsp all-purpose flour

1 cup beef or chicken stock

$^1/_2$ cup full-bodied red wine

Worcestershire sauce (optional)

salt and pepper

MASHED POTATOES

1 lb 8 oz/675 g mealy potatoes,
peeled and cut into chunks

4 tbsp butter

2 tbsp cream or milk

salt and pepper

Preheat the oven to 350°F/180°C. Heat the oil in a large casserole over medium heat. Add the onions and cook, stirring frequently, for 5 minutes, or until softened. Stir in the garlic. Increase the heat, add the ground meat, and cook, stirring constantly with a wooden spoon to break up the meat, until browned all over. Add the carrots and season well with salt and pepper.

Stir in the flour and add the stock and wine. Bring to a boil, stirring, then reduce the heat and simmer until thickened.

Cover the casserole, transfer to the preheated oven, and cook for 1 hour. Check the consistency from time to time and add a little more stock or wine, if necessary. The meat mixture should be quite thick, but not dry. Season to taste with salt and pepper and add a little Worcestershire sauce, if you like.

Meanwhile, cook the potatoes in a large pan of boiling salted water for 15–20 minutes, then drain well. Mash with a potato masher until smooth. Beat in the butter and cream and season well with salt and pepper.

Spoon the lamb mixture into an ovenproof serving dish and spread or pipe the potato on top.

Increase the oven temperature to 400°F/200°C and bake the pie at the top of the oven for 15–20 minutes until golden brown. Finish off under a medium broiler for a really crisp brown potato topping.

POTATO, BEEF, AND LEEK PARCELS

Preheat the oven to 400°F/200°C. Lightly grease a cookie sheet. Mix the potatoes, carrot, beef, and leek together in a large bowl. Season well with salt and pepper.

Divide the pastry into 4 equal-size pieces. Roll out each piece on a lightly floured counter into an 8-inch/20-cm circle.

Spoon the potato mixture onto one half of each circle, to within 1/2 inch/1 cm of the edge. Top the potato mixture with the butter, dividing it equally between the circles. Brush the pastry edge with a little of the beaten egg. Fold the pastry over to encase the filling and crimp the edges together to seal.

Transfer the parcels to the prepared cookie sheet and brush with the beaten egg to glaze.

Bake in the preheated oven for 20 minutes. Reduce the temperature to 325°F/160°C and bake for an additional 30 minutes, or until golden brown.

Serve the parcels hot or warm.

SERVES 4

butter, for greasing

8 oz/225 g waxy potatoes, diced

1 small carrot, diced

8 oz/225 g beef steak, cubed

1 leek, sliced

8 oz/225 g ready-made short-crust pastry, thawed if frozen

all-purpose flour, for dusting

1 tbsp butter

1 egg, beaten

salt and pepper

USE OTHER TYPES OF MEAT, SUCH AS PORK OR CHICKEN, IN THE PARCELS AND ADD CHUNKS OF APPLE TO THE FILLING, IF PREFERRED.

CARROT-TOPPED BEEF PIE

SERVES 4

1 lb/450 g fresh ground beef

1 onion, chopped

1 garlic clove, crushed

1 tbsp all-purpose flour

1¼ cups beef stock

2 tbsp tomato paste

1 celery stalk, chopped

3 tbsp chopped fresh parsley

1 tbsp Worcestershire sauce

1 lb 8 oz/675 g mealy potatoes, diced

2 large carrots, diced

2 tbsp butter

3 tbsp milk

salt and pepper

Heat a large pan over high heat. Add the ground beef and dry-fry for 3–4 minutes, stirring constantly with a wooden spoon to break up the meat, until browned all over. Add the onion and garlic and cook, stirring frequently, for 5 minutes, or until the onion is softened.

Add the flour and cook, stirring, for 1 minute. Gradually blend in the stock and tomato paste. Stir in the celery, 1 tablespoon of the parsley, and the Worcestershire sauce. Season to taste with salt and pepper.

Bring the mixture to a boil, then reduce the heat and simmer for 20–25 minutes. Spoon into a 1-quart pie dish. Preheat the oven to 375°F/190°C.

Meanwhile, cook the potatoes and carrots in a pan of boiling water for 10 minutes. Drain and mash them together.

Beat the butter, milk, and the remaining parsley into the potato and carrot mixture and season to taste with salt and pepper. Spread

or pipe the potato and carrot mixture on top of the meat mixture.

Bake in the preheated oven for 45 minutes, or until cooked through and golden brown on top. Serve hot.

You can use fresh ground lamb, turkey, or pork instead of the beef, adding appropriate herbs, such as rosemary and sage, for added flavor.

STEAK AND KIDNEY PIE

Preheat the oven to 325°F/160°C. Grease a 1-quart pie dish.

Put the flour with salt and pepper to taste in a large plastic bag, add the steak and kidneys, and shake well to coat each piece.

Heat the oil in an ovenproof casserole over high heat. Add the steak and kidneys, in batches, and cook until browned all over. Remove with a slotted spoon and keep warm. Add the onion and garlic to the casserole and cook, stirring, for 2–3 minutes until softened.

Stir in the wine and scrape the sediment from the bottom of the casserole. Pour in the stock and bring to a boil, stirring constantly. Let bubble for 2–3 minutes. Add the bay leaf and return the meat to the casserole.

Cover, transfer to the center of the preheated oven, and cook for $1^1/_2$–2 hours. Taste and adjust the seasoning, if necessary. Let cool, then preferably let chill overnight to develop the flavors. Remove the bay leaf.

Preheat the oven to 400°F/200°C. Roll out the pastry on a lightly floured counter to about $2^3/_4$ inches/ 7 cm larger than the pie dish. Cut off a $1^1/_4$-inch/3-cm strip from the edge. Moisten the rim of the dish and press the pastry strip onto it. Put a pie funnel in the center of the dish and spoon in the steak and kidney filling. Don't overfill—and keep any extra gravy to serve separately. Moisten the pastry collar with water and put on the pastry lid. Crimp the edges of the pastry firmly. Brush with the beaten egg to glaze.

Bake the pie on a cookie sheet near the top of the preheated oven for 30 minutes, or until golden brown and the filling is bubbling hot. Cover with foil and reduce the oven temperature a little if the pastry is getting too brown.

SERVES 4–6

butter, for greasing

2 tbsp all-purpose flour, plus extra for dusting

1 lb 9 oz/700 g top round steak, trimmed and cut into $1^1/_2$-inch/ 4-cm cubes

3 lamb's kidneys, skinned, cored, and cut into 1-inch/ 2.5-cm pieces

3 tbsp vegetable oil

1 onion, coarsely chopped

1 garlic clove, finely chopped

$^1/_2$ cup full-bodied red wine

2 cups stock

1 bay leaf

14 oz/400 g ready-made puff pastry, thawed if frozen

1 egg, beaten

salt and pepper

SOME PEOPLE USE SHORT-CRUST PASTRY FOR THIS PIE, BUT THE RICHER PUFF PASTRY IS BETTER AS IT GIVES A REALLY CRISP CRUST WHILE ALLOWING THE BASE OF THE PASTRY TO ABSORB SOME OF THE GRAVY AND HENCE HAVE A BETTER FLAVOR. THERE ARE REGIONAL VARIATIONS OF STEAK AND KIDNEY PIE, WITH SOME COOKS ADDING MUSHROOMS AND OYSTERS TO THE FILLING.

BEEF IN PUFF PASTRY

SERVES 4

1 lb 10 oz/750 g thick beef tenderloin

2 tbsp butter

2 tbsp vegetable oil

1 garlic clove, chopped

1 onion, chopped

6 oz/175 g cremini mushrooms

1 tbsp chopped fresh sage

12 oz/350 g ready-made puff pastry, thawed if frozen

all-purpose flour, for dusting

1 egg, beaten

salt and pepper

Preheat the oven to 425°F/220°C. Put the beef in a roasting pan, spread with the butter, and season to taste with salt and pepper. Roast in the preheated oven for 30 minutes. Meanwhile, heat the oil in a pan over medium heat. Add the garlic and onion and cook, stirring, for 3 minutes. Add the mushrooms, sage, and salt and pepper to taste and cook, stirring frequently, for 5 minutes. Remove from the heat.

Roll out the pastry on a lightly floured counter into a rectangle large enough to enclose the beef. Put the beef in the center and spread over the mushroom mixture. Bring the long sides of the pastry together over the beef and seal with the beaten egg. Tuck the short ends over (trim away the excess pastry) and seal. Put, seam-side down, on a cookie sheet. Make 2 slits in the top. Decorate with pastry trimmings and brush with the beaten egg to glaze.

Bake in the oven for 40 minutes. Cut into thick slices to serve.

STEAK AND MUSHROOM PIE

Preheat the oven to 325°F/160°C. Put 2 tablespoons of the flour in a large plastic bag with salt and pepper to taste, add the meat, and shake well to coat each piece.

Heat the oil in an ovenproof casserole over high heat and cook the meat until brown. Brown the meat in batches. Remove it from the dish with a slotted spoon and keep it warm.

Fry the onion and garlic in the casserole dish over medium heat for 2–3 minutes until softened and then add the mushrooms. Continue to cook for about 2 minutes, stirring constantly, until they start to shrink.

Carefully stir in the wine and scrape the bottom of the pan to release all the sediment. Pour in the stock, stirring constantly, and bring to a boil—let the mixture simmer for 2–3 minutes.

Add the bay leaf and return the meat to the casserole. Cover and cook in the center of the preheated oven for 1½–2 hours until the meat is tender. Check the seasoning and adjust if necessary.

Remove from the oven, discard the bay leaf, and cool before chilling in a refrigerator, preferably overnight (to let the flavors develop).

Preheat the oven to 400°F/200°C. Roll out the pastry on a lightly floured counter to about 2 inches/5 cm larger than the pie dish (use the inverted dish as a measure). Cut off a strip, ½ inch/1 cm wide, from around the edge. Moisten the rim of the dish with water and press the pastry strip onto it. Place a pie funnel in the center of the dish and spoon in the steak and mushroom filling. Do not overfill, and keep any extra gravy to serve separately.

Moisten the pastry collar with a little water and put on the pastry lid, taking care to fit it carefully round the pie funnel. Crimp the edges of the pastry firmly and glaze with the beaten egg. You can use some leftover dough to make leaf shapes to garnish the pie—stick these on using the beaten egg and glaze well with egg.

Place the pie on a cookie sheet and bake near the top of the preheated oven for 30 minutes, or until golden brown. If the pastry is getting too brown, cover it with foil and reduce the oven temperature to 350°F/180°C. The pie should be golden brown and the filling bubbling hot.

SERVES 4–6

4 tbsp all-purpose flour

1 lb 9 oz/700 g top round steak, cut into 1½ inch/4 cm pieces

3 tbsp vegetable oil

1 onion, coarsely chopped

1 garlic clove, finely chopped

12 oz/350 g mushrooms, wiped and sliced

½ cup full-bodied red wine

2 cups beef stock

1 bay leaf

14 oz/400 g ready-made puff pastry, thawed if frozen

1 egg, beaten

salt and pepper

8

BARBECUES

Cook over a barbecue to enjoy the natural flavors of meat at its best, when the mild smokiness and caramelized meat sugars simply melt in your mouth. All types of meat can be cooked on a barbecue but, just as with other fast cooking techniques such as broiling or frying, the cuts that work best are steaks, cubed lean meat, chops, sausages, and burgers. The golden rule of barbecuing is always to cook over embers rather than flames—this stops the meat from becoming unpleasantly carbonized. Try out Sherried Chicken Liver Brochettes, Duck with Apricots, or Turkish Kabobs for a delicious change from steaks and sausages.

SPICY CHICKEN KABOBS

Put the chicken cubes in a large, shallow, nonmetallic dish. Put the oil, lemon rind and juice, garlic, and chiles in a pitcher and stir together until well blended. Season to taste with salt and pepper. Pour over the chicken and turn gently to coat in the marinade. Cover and let marinate in the refrigerator for up to 8 hours.

Preheat the barbecue. Remove the chicken from the marinade, setting aside the marinade. Thread the chicken onto several presoaked wooden skewers and cook over medium-hot coals, turning frequently and brushing with the marinade, but not for the last 5 minutes of the cooking time, for 10 minutes, or until the chicken is cooked through.

Transfer to a large serving dish, garnish with parsley sprigs, and serve immediately.

SERVES 4

4 skinless, boneless chicken breasts, about 6 oz/175 g each, cut into 1-inch/2.5-cm cubes

$^{1}/_{2}$ cup olive oil

finely grated rind and juice of 1 lemon

2 garlic cloves, finely chopped

2 tsp finely chopped fresh red chiles

salt and pepper

fresh flat-leaf parsley sprigs, to garnish

SHERRIED CHICKEN LIVER BROCHETTES

Cut the chicken livers into 2-inch/ 5-cm pieces. Combine the ingredients for the marinade in a shallow dish. Add the chicken livers and toss to coat in the marinade. Cover and let marinate in the refrigerator for 3–4 hours.

Mix the mustard and mayonnaise together in a bowl, cover, and let chill until required.

Preheat the barbecue. Cut each bacon strip in half. Put on a cutting board and use the back of a knife to stretch gently until almost double in length. Remove the chicken livers from the marinade, setting aside the marinade. Wrap the bacon strip around half of the chicken liver pieces. Thread the bacon and chicken liver rolls and the plain chicken liver pieces alternately onto 6 presoaked wooden skewers.

Cook over hot coals, turning frequently and brushing with the marinade, but not for the last 5 minutes of the cooking time, for 10–12 minutes until cooked through.

Meanwhile, cut each bread half into 3 pieces and toast the cut sides on the barbecue until golden brown.

To serve, top the toasted bread with the spinach and put the kabobs on top. Spoon over the mayonnaise.

SERVES 6

14 oz/400 g chicken livers, cored and trimmed

3 rindless lean bacon strips

1 ciabatta loaf or small French stick, halved horizontally

5 cups baby spinach leaves, washed

MARINADE

$^2/_3$ cup dry sherry

4 tbsp olive oil

1 tsp whole grain mustard

salt and pepper, to taste

MUSTARD MAYONNAISE

8 tbsp mayonnaise

1 tsp whole grain mustard

TAKE CARE NOT TO OVERCOOK THE CHICKEN LIVERS OR THEY WILL BECOME TOUGH. THEY SHOULD BE FIRM TO THE TOUCH AND JUST PINK INSIDE.

BARBECUED CHICKEN

SERVES 4

4 cups chicken stock

8 chicken thighs

1 tbsp lime juice

2 garlic cloves, crushed

2 tbsp Thai soy sauce

1 tbsp Thai fish sauce

2 tbsp chili sauce

lime wedges, to garnish

Bring the stock to a boil in a large wok or pan. Add the chicken, reduce the heat, and simmer for 8–10 minutes until cooked. Remove with a slotted spoon and let cool.

When cold, put the chicken in a shallow, nonmetallic dish. Combine the lime juice, garlic, soy sauce, fish sauce, and chili sauce in a bowl and spoon over the chicken, turning to coat in the marinade. Cover and let marinate in the refrigerator for 2–3 hours. Preheat the barbecue.

Remove the chicken from the marinade, reserving the marinade. Cook the chicken over hot coals, turning frequently and brushing with the marinade, but not for the last 5 minutes of the cooking time, for 8–10 minutes until browned and crisp. Serve the chicken hot or cold, garnished with lime wedges.

YOU CAN ALSO COOK THE CHICKEN UNDER THE BROILER OR ON A RIDGED GRILL PAN. IT IS IMPORTANT THAT THE MEAT IS COOKED ALL THE WAY THROUGH—THIS IS WHY IT IS COOKED BEFORE BARBECUING. DON'T FORGET THAT REHEATING MEAT THOROUGHLY IS JUST AS IMPORTANT AS COOKING IT THOROUGHLY.

CAJUN CHICKEN

SERVES 4

4 chicken drumsticks

4 chicken thighs

2 fresh corncob, husks and silks removed

6 tbsp butter, melted

SPICE MIX

2 tsp onion powder

2 tsp paprika

$1\frac{1}{2}$ tsp salt

1 tsp garlic powder

1 tsp dried thyme

1 tsp cayenne pepper

1 tsp ground black pepper

$\frac{1}{2}$ tsp ground white pepper

$\frac{1}{4}$ tsp ground cumin

Preheat the barbecue. Using a sharp knife, make 2 or 3 diagonal slashes in the chicken drumsticks and thighs, then put in a large dish. Cut the corncob into thick slices and add to the dish. Mix all the ingredients for the spice mix together in a small bowl.

Brush the chicken and corn with the melted butter and sprinkle with the spice mix. Toss to coat well.

Cook the chicken over medium-hot coals, turning occasionally, for 15 minutes, then add the corn slices and cook, turning occasionally, for an additional 10–15 minutes, or until beginning to blacken slightly at the edges. Transfer to a large serving plate and serve immediately.

TO REMOVE THE HUSKS FROM THE CORNCOB, GENTLY PULL THEM AWAY FROM THE CORN TOWARD THE BASE, THEN CUT OFF THE BASE AND REMOVE THE SILKS.

LEMON SQUAB CHICKENS

Preheat the barbecue. To spatchcock the squab chickens, turn one bird breast-side down, and, using strong kitchen scissors or poultry shears, cut through the skin and ribcage along both sides of the backbone, from tail to neck. Remove the backbone and turn the bird breast-side up. Press down firmly on the breastbone with the heel of your hand to flatten. Fold the wingtips underneath. Repeat with the remaining squab chickens.

Thinly slice half the lemon and finely grate the rind of the other half. Mix the lemon rind and sage together in a small bowl. Loosen the skin on the breasts and legs of the squab chickens and insert the lemon and sage mixture. Tuck in the lemon slices and smooth the skin back firmly. Push a metal skewer through one wing, the top of the breast and the other wing. Push a second skewer through one thigh, the bottom of the breast and the other thigh. Season to taste with salt and pepper.

Cook the squab chickens over medium-hot coals for 10–15 minutes on each side. Serve garnished with herb sprigs and lemon slices.

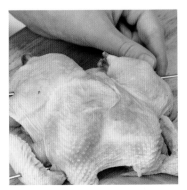

SERVES 4

4 squab chickens, about 1 lb/
450 g each

1 lemon

2 tbsp chopped fresh sage

salt and pepper

TO GARNISH

fresh herb sprigs

lemon slices

YOU CAN THREAD THE SKEWERS CROSSWISE THROUGH THE SQUAB CHICKEN. PUSH A SKEWER THROUGH A WING AND OUT THROUGH THE THIGH ON THE OPPOSITE SIDE. REPEAT WITH THE OTHER SKEWER ON THE OTHER SIDE.

DUCK WITH APRICOTS

SERVES 4

4 duck breasts, about 6 oz/
175 g each

²/₃ cup no-soak dried apricots

2 shallots, thinly sliced

2 tbsp honey

1 tsp sesame oil

2 tsp Chinese five-spice powder

4 scallion tassels, to garnish

Preheat the barbecue. Using a sharp knife, cut a long slit in the fleshy side of each duck breast to make a pocket. Divide the apricots and shallots between the pockets and secure with skewers.

Mix the honey and sesame oil together in a small bowl and brush all over the duck breasts. Sprinkle the duck breasts all over with the five-spice powder.

To make the garnish, make a few cuts lengthwise down each scallion. Put in a bowl of iced water and leave until the tassels open out. Drain well before using.

Cook the duck breasts over medium-hot coals for 6–8 minutes on each side. Remove the skewers, transfer to a large serving plate, and garnish with the scallion tassels. Serve immediately.

SPICY TURKEY AND CHORIZO KABOBS

Put the oil, garlic, chile, and salt and pepper to taste in a small screw-top jar, screw the lid on tightly, and shake well to combine. Let stand for 1 hour for the garlic and chili to flavor the oil.

Preheat the barbecue. Using a sharp knife, cut the turkey into 1-inch/2.5-cm pieces. Cut the chorizo into 1-inch/2.5-cm lengths. Core the apple and cut into chunks. Sprinkle the apple with the lemon juice to prevent discoloration.

Thread the turkey and chorizo pieces onto 8 metal skewers, alternating with the apple chunks and bay leaves.

Cook the kabobs over hot coals, turning and basting frequently with the flavored oil, for 15 minutes, or until the turkey is cooked through.

Transfer the kabobs to warmed serving plates and serve immediately.

SERVES 8

6 tbsp olive oil

2 garlic cloves, crushed

1 fresh red chile, seeded and chopped

12 oz/350 g turkey breast fillet

10$^{1}/_{2}$ oz/300 g chorizo sausage

1 eating apple

1 tbsp lemon juice

8 bay leaves

salt and pepper

THE FLAVORED OIL FEATURED IN THIS RECIPE CAN BE USED TO BASTE ANY GRILLED MEAT, GIVING IT A SUBTLE CHILE FLAVOR. IT WILL KEEP IN THE REFRIGERATOR FOR ABOUT 2 WEEKS.

CHINESE RIBS

Put the spareribs in a large, shallow, nonmetallic dish. Mix the soy sauce, sugar, oil, garlic, five-spice powder, and ginger together in a bowl. Pour the mixture over the ribs and turn until coated in the marinade. Cover and let marinate in the refrigerator for at least 6 hours.

Preheat the barbecue. Remove the ribs from the marinade, setting aside the marinade. Cook over medium-hot coals, turning frequently and brushing with the reserved marinade, but not for the last 10 minutes of the cooking time, for 30–40 minutes.

Transfer to a large serving dish, garnish with the shredded scallions, and serve immediately.

SERVES 4

2 lb 4 oz/1 kg pork spareribs, separated

4 tbsp dark soy sauce

3 tbsp brown sugar

1 tbsp peanut or sunflower-seed oil

2 garlic cloves, finely chopped

2 tsp Chinese five-spice powder

$1/2$-inch/1-cm piece fresh gingerroot, grated

shredded scallions, to garnish

SAUSAGES IN BACON

Preheat the barbecue. Thinly slice the mozzarella cheese. Using a sharp knife, cut a deep slit in the side of each sausage. Spread the cut sides with the mustard. Divide the slices of cheese between the sausages and reshape.

Put the bacon strips on a cutting board and use the back of a knife to stretch gently until almost double in length. Wrap one strip tightly around each sausage.

Cook over hot coals, turning frequently, for 15–20 minutes until cooked through. Transfer to a large serving plate and serve immediately.

SERVES 4

4 oz/115 g mozzarella cheese

8 sausages

2 tbsp Dijon mustard

8 smoked bacon strips

PORK BROCHETTES

Using a sharp knife, cut the pork into 1-inch/2.5-cm cubes, then put in a large, shallow, nonmetallic dish. Mix the cider, sage, and peppercorns together in a pitcher, pour over the pork cubes, and turn to coat in the marinade. Cover and let marinate in the refrigerator for 1–2 hours.

Preheat the barbecue. Remove the pork from the marinade, setting aside the marinade. Core the apples, but do not peel, and cut into wedges. Dip the apple wedges into the reserved marinade and thread onto several metal skewers, alternating with the cubes of pork. Stir the sunflower-seed oil into the remaining marinade.

Cook the brochettes over medium-hot coals, turning frequently and brushing with the marinade, but not for the last 5 minutes of the cooking time, for 12–15 minutes. Transfer to a large serving plate and serve immediately.

SERVES 4

1 lb/450 g pork tenderloin

1¼ cups hard cider

1 tbsp finely chopped fresh sage

6 black peppercorns, crushed

2 crisp eating apples

1 tbsp sunflower-seed oil

REPLACE 1 APPLE WITH 6 NO-SOAK PRUNES WRAPPED IN STRIPS OF LEAN BACON. THREAD THE PRUNES ONTO THE SKEWERS WITH THE REMAINING APPLE AND PORK.

SAUSAGES WITH BARBECUE SAUCE

To make the sauce, heat the oil in a small pan over medium heat. Add the onion and garlic and cook, stirring frequently, for 4–5 minutes until the onion is softened.

Add the tomatoes with their juice, the Worcestershire sauce, brown fruity sauce, sugar, vinegar, chili powder, mustard powder, Tabasco sauce, and salt and pepper to taste. Bring to a boil, stirring.

Reduce the heat to low and simmer gently, stirring occasionally, for 10–15 minutes, or until beginning to thicken slightly. Keep warm until required.

Preheat the barbecue. Cook the sausages over hot coals, turning frequently, for 10–15 minutes until cooked through. Do not prick the sausages with a fork or the juices and fat will run out and cause the barbecue to flare.

Put each sausage in a hotdog bun and serve immediately with the barbecue sauce.

SERVES 4

2 tbsp sunflower-seed oil

1 large onion, chopped

2 garlic cloves, chopped

8 oz/225 g canned chopped tomatoes in juice

1 tbsp Worcestershire sauce

2 tbsp brown fruity sauce

2 tbsp brown sugar

4 tbsp white wine vinegar

1/2 tsp mild chili powder

1/4 tsp mustard powder

dash of Tabasco sauce

1 lb/450 g sausages

salt and pepper

hotdog buns, to serve

TURKISH KABOBS

SERVES 4

1 lb 2 oz/500 g boned
shoulder of lamb, cut into
1-inch/2.5-cm cubes

1 tbsp olive oil

2 tbsp dry white wine

2 tbsp finely chopped
fresh mint

4 garlic cloves, finely chopped

2 tsp grated orange rind

1 tbsp paprika

1 tsp sugar

salt and pepper

SESAME SEED CREAM

8 oz/225 g sesame seed paste

2 garlic cloves, finely chopped

2 tbsp extra virgin olive oil

2 tbsp lemon juice

1/2 cup water

Put the lamb cubes in a large, shallow, nonmetallic dish. Mix the oil, wine, mint, garlic, orange rind, paprika, and sugar together in a pitcher and season with salt and pepper. Pour over the lamb and turn to coat in the marinade. Cover and let marinate in the refrigerator for 2 hours, turning occasionally.

Preheat the barbecue. To make the sesame seed cream, put the sesame seed paste, garlic, oil, and lemon juice in a food processor and process briefly to mix. With the motor still running, gradually add the water through the feed tube until smooth. Transfer to a bowl, cover, and let chill until required.

Remove the lamb from the marinade, setting aside the marinade. Thread onto several long metal skewers. Cook over medium-hot coals, turning frequently and brushing with the marinade, but not for the last 5 minutes of the cooking time, for 10–15 minutes, or until cooked through.

Serve the kabobs immediately with the sesame seed cream.

SESAME SEED PASTE IS AVAILABLE FROM MOST SUPERMARKETS AND SPECIALIST FOOD STORES. IT IS MADE FROM GROUND, PULPED SESAME SEEDS.

SPICY RACK OF LAMB WITH HUMMUS

Preheat the oven to 375°F/190°C. Put the lamb in a roasting pan and spoon over the oil. Roast in the preheated oven for 10–15 minutes, or until almost cooked through.

Mix all the ingredients for the marinade together in a small bowl. Brush the spice mixture all over the warm lamb, then transfer to a dish and let cool completely. Cover and let marinate in the refrigerator overnight.

Preheat the barbecue. Cook the lamb over medium-hot coals, turning frequently, until heated through and well browned. Transfer to 6 serving plates and add 2–3 tablespoons hummus to each. Garnish with mint sprigs and serve.

SERVES 6

6 racks of lamb, each with 3 chops

2 tbsp olive oil

few fresh mint sprigs, to garnish

ready-made hummus, to serve

MARINADE

1 tbsp olive oil

2 tbsp honey

2 tsp ground coriander

2 tsp ground cumin

1 tsp ground allspice

$\frac{1}{2}$ tsp paprika

HAMBURGERS WITH CHILE AND BASIL

SERVES 4

1 lb 7 oz/650 g fresh ground beef

1 red bell pepper, seeded and finely chopped

1 garlic clove, finely chopped

2 small fresh red chiles, seeded, and finely chopped

1 tbsp chopped fresh basil, plus extra sprigs to garnish

$1/2$ tsp ground cumin

salt and pepper

hamburger buns, to serve

Preheat the barbecue. Put the ground beef, red bell pepper, garlic, chiles, chopped basil, and cumin in a bowl and mix until well combined. Season the mixture to taste with salt and pepper.

With wet hands, form the mixture into burger shapes. Cook the burgers over hot coals for 5–8 minutes on each side, or until cooked through.

Serve immediately in hamburger buns, garnished with basil sprigs.

MUSTARD STEAKS WITH TOMATO RELISH

To make the tomato relish, put all the ingredients in a heavy-bottom pan and season to taste with salt. Bring to a boil, stirring until the sugar has completely dissolved. Reduce the heat and simmer, stirring occasionally, for 40 minutes, or until thickened. Transfer to a bowl, cover, and let cool.

Preheat the barbecue. Using a sharp knife, cut almost completely through each steak horizontally to make a pocket. Spread the mustard inside the pockets and rub the

steaks all over with the garlic. Put on a plate, cover, and let stand in a cool place for 30 minutes.

Cook the steaks over hot coals for 2¹/₂ minutes each side for rare, 4 minutes each side for medium, or 6 minutes each side for well done.

Transfer to warmed serving plates, garnish with tarragon sprigs, and serve immediately with the tomato relish.

SERVES 4

4 sirloin or rump steaks

1 tbsp tarragon mustard

2 garlic cloves, crushed

fresh tarragon sprigs, to garnish

TOMATO RELISH

8 oz/225 g cherry tomatoes

generous ¹/₄ cup brown sugar

¹/₄ cup white wine vinegar

1 piece preserved ginger, chopped

¹/₂ lime, thinly sliced

salt

USE LONG-HANDLED TONGS TO TURN THE STEAKS OVER. TRY TO AVOID USING A FORK, AS THIS WILL PIERCE THE MEAT AND SOME OF THE DELICIOUS JUICES WILL BE LOST.

BEEF SATAY

Using a sharp knife, cut the steak into 1-inch/2.5-cm cubes, then put in a large, shallow, nonmetallic dish. Mix the honey, soy sauce, oil, garlic, coriander, caraway seeds, and chili powder together in a small pitcher. Pour over the steak and turn to coat in the marinade. Cover and let marinate in the refrigerator for 2 hours, turning occasionally. Preheat the barbecue.

Remove the steak from the marinade, setting aside the marinade. Thread onto several presoaked wooden skewers.

Cook over hot coals, turning frequently and brushing with the marinade, but not for the last 5 minutes of the cooking time, for 8 minutes, or until cooked through. Transfer to a large serving plate, garnish with lime wedges, and serve.

SERVES 6

2 lb 4 oz/1 kg rump steak

1 tbsp honey

2 tbsp dark soy sauce

2 tbsp peanut oil

1 garlic clove, finely chopped

1 tsp ground coriander

1 tsp caraway seeds

pinch of chili powder

lime wedges, to garnish

INSTEAD OF CUTTING THE STEAK INTO SMALL CUBES, SLICE IT INTO LONG, NARROW STRIPS AND THREAD THE STRIPS CONCERTINA-STYLE ONTO THE SKEWERS.

THAI-SPICED BEEF AND PEPPER KABOBS

SERVES 4

4 tbsp rice wine or dry sherry

generous $^1/_4$ cup soy sauce

generous $^1/_4$ cup hoisin sauce

3 garlic cloves, finely chopped

1 fresh red chile, seeded and finely chopped

$1^1/_2$ tbsp grated fresh gingerroot

3 scallions, finely chopped

salt and pepper

KABOBS

2 lb 4 oz/1 kg rump or sirloin steak, cubed

2 large red bell peppers, seeded and cut into small chunks

green and red lettuce leaves, to serve

Put the rice wine, soy sauce, hoisin sauce, garlic, chile, ginger, and scallions in a large bowl and mix until well combined. Season to taste with salt and pepper.

Thread the meat onto 8 metal skewers, alternating with chunks of red bell pepper, leaving a small space at either end.

Transfer the skewers to the bowl and turn to coat in the marinade. Cover and let marinate in the refrigerator for at least $2^1/_2$ hours or overnight.

Preheat the barbecue. Remove the skewers from the marinade and cook over hot coals, turning frequently, for 10–15 minutes, or until the meat is cooked through.

Serve immediately on a bed of green and red lettuce leaves.

MEATBALLS ON STICKS

SERVES 8

4 pork and herb sausages

$1/2$ cup fresh ground beef

$1^1/2$ cups fresh white bread crumbs

1 onion, finely chopped

2 tbsp chopped mixed fresh herbs, such as parsley, thyme, and sage

1 egg

salt and pepper

sunflower-seed oil, for brushing

sauces of your choice, to serve

Preheat the barbecue. Remove the sausage meat from the skins of the sausages, put in a large bowl, and break up with a fork. Add the ground beef, bread crumbs, onion, herbs, and egg. Season the mixture to taste with salt and pepper and stir well with a wooden spoon until thoroughly blended.

Shape the mixture into small balls, about the size of golf balls, between the palms of your hands. Spear each one with a wooden toothpick and brush with oil.

Cook over medium-hot coals, turning frequently and brushing with more oil as necessary, for 10 minutes, or until cooked through. Transfer to a large serving plate and serve immediately with a choice of sauces.

AN INCREASING NUMBER OF FLAVORED SAUSAGES ARE AVAILABLE, FROM LEEK AND BLACK PEPPER TO CHILE, AND CAN BE USED FOR THESE MEATBALLS.

9

ACCOMPANIMENTS

Meat benefits from numerous trimmings, from sauces and stuffings to vegetables and potatoes. Find out how to cook potatoes to crisp, golden perfection, or how to make Chestnut and Sausage Stuffing, Quick Horseradish or Mint Sauce, or traditional gravies. A good marinade can transform an otherwise dull piece of meat into something quite extraordinary—check out the citrus and herb marinades or Honey Mustard Marinade for delicious combinations to tantalize your taste buds.

APRICOT, QUICK HORSERADISH, AND MINT SAUCES

To make the Apricot Sauce, put the apricots and syrup into a food processor or blender and process until smooth.

Pour the purée into a pan, add the other ingredients, and mix together well. Heat over low heat for 4–5 minutes until warm. Remove from the heat and pour into a serving pitcher. This sauce goes well with ham.

To make the Quick Horseradish Sauce, mix the horseradish and sour cream together in a small bowl until well blended. Serve the sauce with roast beef.

To make the Mint Sauce, make sure that the mint is clean and tear the leaves from their stems. If the mint is dirty, wash it gently and dry thoroughly before tearing off the leaves.

Put the leaves on a cutting board and sprinkle with the sugar. Chop the leaves finely (the sugar helps the chopping process) and put in a small heatproof bowl. Pour over the boiling water and stir until the sugar has dissolved.

Stir in the vinegar, then cover and let stand for 30 minutes. Garnish with a mint leaf. This sauce goes particularly well with roast lamb.

SERVES 6

APRICOT SAUCE

14 oz/400 g canned apricot halves in syrup

$^2/_3$ cup vegetable stock

$^1/_2$ cup Marsala

$^1/_2$ tsp ground ginger

$^1/_2$ tsp ground cinnamon

salt and pepper

QUICK HORSERADISH SAUCE

6 tbsp creamed horseradish sauce

6 tbsp sour cream

MINT SAUCE

small bunch of fresh mint

2 tsp superfine sugar

2 tbsp boiling water

2 tbsp white wine vinegar

fresh mint leaf, to garnish

CRANBERRY SAUCE

Cut the strips of lemon and orange rind into thin shreds and put in a heavy-bottomed pan.

If using fresh cranberries, rinse well and remove any stalks. Add the cranberries, citrus juice, and sugar to the pan and cook over medium heat, stirring occasionally, for 5 minutes, or until the cranberries are beginning to burst.

Strain the juice into a clean pan and set aside the cranberries. Stir the arrowroot mixture into the juice, then bring to a boil, stirring constantly, until the sauce is smooth and thickened. Remove from the heat and stir in the reserved cranberries.

Transfer the sauce to a bowl and let cool, then cover and let chill in the refrigerator.

SERVES 8

thinly pared rind and juice of 1 lemon

thinly pared rind and juice of 1 orange

12 oz/350 g cranberries, thawed if frozen

$^3/_4$ cup superfine sugar

2 tbsp arrowroot blended with 3 tbsp cold water

TRADITIONAL GRAVIES

To make the Chicken Gravy, blend the cornstarch with the water in a pitcher, then stir into the juices in the roasting pan. Put the roasting pan over low heat and cook, stirring, until thickened. Add more water, if necessary. Season to taste with salt and pepper.

To make the Beef Gravy, pour off most of the fat from the roasting pan, leaving behind the meat juices and the sediment. Put the roasting pan over medium heat and scrape all the sediment from the bottom of the pan. Sprinkle in the flour and quickly mix it into the juices with a small whisk. When you have a smooth paste, gradually add the wine and most of the stock, whisking constantly. Bring to a boil, then reduce the heat to a gentle simmer and cook for 2–3 minutes. Season to taste with salt and pepper and add the remaining stock, if necessary, and a little Worcestershire sauce, if you like.

SERVES 4

CHICKEN GRAVY

1 tbsp cornstarch

2 tbsp water

pan juices from
a chicken roasting pan

salt and pepper

BEEF GRAVY

pan juices from a meat
roasting pan

3 tbsp all-purpose flour

1^{1}/$_{4}$ cups red wine

1^{1}/$_{4}$ cups beef stock

Worcestershire sauce (optional)

salt and pepper

MUSHROOM STUFFING

SERVES 6–8

4 tbsp butter

3 shallots, chopped

8 oz/225 g mixed wild and cultivated mushrooms, chopped

4 oz/115 g pork sausage meat

1$\frac{1}{2}$ cups fresh white bread crumbs

few drops of truffle oil (optional)

salt and pepper

Melt the butter in a heavy-bottomed skillet over low heat. Add the shallots and cook, stirring occasionally, for 5 minutes, or until softened. Add the mushrooms and cook, stirring occasionally, until their juices have evaporated.

Transfer the shallots and mushrooms to a bowl, add the sausage meat, bread crumbs, and truffle oil, if using, and season to taste with salt and pepper. Mix together well.

If you are planning to stuff a turkey or goose, fill only the neck cavity. It is safer and more reliable to cook the stuffing separately, either rolled into small balls and put on a cookie sheet or spooned into an ovenproof dish.

Cook the separate stuffing in a preheated oven at 375°F/190°C for 30–40 minutes. Allow a longer cooking time if you are roasting a bird at a lower temperature in the same oven.

CHESTNUT AND SAUSAGE STUFFING

Mix the sausage meat and chestnut purée together in a bowl, then stir in the walnuts, apricots, parsley, chives, and sage. Stir in enough of the cream to make a firm, but not dry, mixture. Season to taste with salt and pepper.

If you are planning to stuff a turkey or goose, fill only the neck cavity. It is safer and more reliable to cook the stuffing separately, either rolled into small balls and put on a cookie sheet, or spooned into an ovenproof dish.

Cook the separate stuffing in a preheated oven at 375°F/190°C for 30–40 minutes. Allow a longer cooking time if you are roasting a bird at a lower temperature in the same oven.

SERVES 6–8

8 oz/225 g pork sausage meat

8 oz/225 g unsweetened chestnut purée

$^3/_4$ cup shelled walnuts, chopped

$^2/_3$ cup no-soak dried apricots, chopped

2 tbsp chopped fresh parsley

2 tbsp snipped fresh chives

2 tsp chopped fresh sage

4–5 tbsp heavy cream

salt and pepper

CITRUS AND HERB MARINADES

SERVES 4

ORANGE AND MARJORAM

1 orange

¹/₂ cup olive oil

4 tbsp dry white wine

4 tbsp white wine vinegar

1 tbsp snipped fresh chives

1 tbsp chopped fresh marjoram

salt and pepper

THAI-SPICED LIME

1 lemongrass stalk

finely grated rind and juice of
1 lime

4 tbsp sesame oil

2 tbsp light soy sauce

pinch of ground ginger

1 tbsp chopped fresh cilantro

salt and pepper

BASIL AND LEMON

finely grated rind of 1 lemon

4 tbsp lemon juice

1 tbsp balsamic vinegar

2 tbsp red wine vinegar

2 tbsp extra virgin olive oil

1 tbsp chopped fresh oregano

1 tbsp chopped fresh basil

salt and pepper

To make the Orange and Marjoram Marinade, remove the rind from the orange with a zester, or grate it finely, then squeeze the juice.

Mix the orange rind and juice with all the remaining ingredients in a small, nonmetallic bowl, whisking together to combine.

To make the Thai-Spiced Lime Marinade, bruise the lemongrass by crushing it with a rolling pin. Mix all the remaining ingredients together in a small, nonmetallic bowl, then mix in the lemongrass.

To make the Basil and Lemon Marinade, whisk all the ingredients together in a small, nonmetallic bowl.

Keep the marinades covered with plastic wrap or store in screw-top jars in the refrigerator, ready for using as marinades or bastes.

HONEY MUSTARD MARINADE

Mix all the ingredients, except the oil, together in a small bowl.

Gradually add the oil, whisking constantly, until it is fully absorbed into the mixture.

Use to marinate and baste chicken or pork, especially spareribs.

2 tbsp honey

2 tbsp whole grain mustard

1 tsp ground ginger

1 tsp garlic powder

2 tsp finely chopped fresh rosemary

4 tbsp dark soy sauce

$^{1}/_{4}$ cup olive oil

MINTED YOGURT MARINADE

Crush the garlic with the salt on a cutting board to make a paste. Scrape into a bowl and stir in the mint, yogurt, and cumin, if using.

If you are using the onion, put it in a food processor, together with the yogurt mixture, and process for a few seconds, or until the mixture is coarsely blended.

Use to marinate and baste lamb.

2 garlic cloves, crushed

1 tsp salt

4 tbsp finely chopped fresh mint

1 cup plain yogurt

1 tsp ground cumin, coriander seeds, or ground cinnamon (optional)

1 onion, coarsely chopped (optional)

ROAST SUMMER VEGETABLES

SERVES 4

2 tbsp olive oil

1 fennel bulb

2 red onions

2 beefsteak tomatoes

1 eggplant

2 zucchini

1 yellow bell pepper

1 red bell pepper

1 orange bell pepper

4 garlic cloves, peeled

4 fresh rosemary sprigs

pepper

Preheat the oven to 400°F/200°C.

Brush a large ovenproof dish with a little of the oil. Cut the fennel bulb, onions, and tomatoes into wedges. Slice the eggplant and zucchini thickly, then seed all the bell peppers and cut into chunks. Arrange the vegetables in the dish and tuck the garlic cloves and rosemary sprigs among them. Drizzle with the remaining oil and season to taste with pepper.

Roast the vegetables in the preheated oven for 20–25 minutes, or until tender and beginning to turn golden brown. Turn the vegetables over halfway through the cooking time.

Serve the vegetables straight from the dish or transfer them to a warmed serving plate. Serve as an accompaniment to barbecued or broiled meat and poultry.

ROASTING BRINGS OUT THE FULL FLAVOR AND SWEETNESS OF THE BELL PEPPERS, EGGPLANTS, ZUCCHINI, AND ONIONS.

ROAST ROOT VEGETABLES

SERVES 4–6

3 parsnips, peeled and cut into 2-inch/5-cm pieces

4 baby turnips, quartered

3 carrots, peeled and cut into 2-inch/5-cm pieces

1 lb/450 g butternut squash, peeled and cut into 2-inch/5-cm chunks

1 lb/450 g sweet potato, peeled and cut into 2-inch/5-cm chunks

2 garlic cloves, finely chopped

2 tbsp chopped fresh rosemary

2 tbsp chopped fresh thyme

2 tsp chopped fresh sage

3 tbsp olive oil

salt and pepper

2 tbsp chopped fresh mixed herbs, such as parsley, thyme, and mint, to garnish

Preheat the oven to 425°F/220°C.

Arrange all the vegetables in a single layer in a large roasting pan. Scatter over the garlic and the chopped herbs.

Pour over the oil and season well with the salt and pepper.

Toss all the ingredients together until well mixed and coated with the oil (you can leave them to marinate at this stage to allow the flavors to be absorbed).

Roast the vegetables at the top of the preheated oven for 50–60 minutes until tender and well browned. Turn the vegetables over halfway through the cooking time.

Sprinkle with the mixed herbs to garnish and add a final sprinkling of salt and pepper. Serve with roast meat, poultry, and game.

SHALLOTS OR WEDGES OF RED ONION CAN BE ADDED TO THE ROOT VEGETABLES TO GIVE ADDITIONAL FLAVOR AND TEXTURE. WHOLE CLOVES OF UNPEELED GARLIC ARE ALSO GOOD ROASTED WITH THE OTHER VEGETABLES. YOU CAN THEN SQUEEZE OUT THE CREAMY COOKED GARLIC OVER THE VEGETABLES WHEN EATING THEM.

ROAST POTATOES

Preheat the oven to 425°F/220°C.

Cook the potatoes in a large pan of boiling salted water over medium heat, covered, for 5–7 minutes. They will be firm. Remove from the heat.

Meanwhile, put the drippings in a roasting pan and put in the preheated oven to heat.

Drain the potatoes well and return to the pan. Cover with the lid and firmly shake the pan so that the surface of the potatoes is roughened.

Remove the roasting pan from the oven and carefully tip the potatoes into the hot drippings. Baste until well coated with the drippings.

Roast the potatoes at the top of the preheated oven for 45–50 minutes until browned all over and thoroughly crisp. Turn the potatoes over and baste again only once halfway through the cooking time, otherwise the crunchy edges will be destroyed.

Carefully transfer the potatoes from the roasting pan to a warmed serving dish. Sprinkle with a little salt and serve immediately. Any leftovers are delicious cold.

Serve with roast or broiled meat, poultry, and game.

SERVES 6

3 lb/1.3 kg large mealy potatoes, peeled and cut into even-size chunks

3 tbsp beef drippings, goose fat, duck fat, or olive oil

salt

PERFECT MASHED POTATOES

Peel the potatoes, putting them in cold water as you prepare the remainder to prevent them from turning brown.

Cut the potatoes into even-size chunks and cook in a large pan of boiling salted water over medium heat, covered, for 20–25 minutes until tender. Test with the point of a knife, making sure that you test right to the middle.

Remove the pan from the heat and drain the potatoes. Return the potatoes to the hot pan and mash with a potato masher until smooth.

Add the butter and continue to mash until it is thoroughly incorporated, then add the hot milk (it is better hot because the potatoes absorb it more quickly to produce a creamier mash).

Season to taste with salt and pepper and serve immediately as an accompaniment to thick casseroles, braised dishes or broiled meat and poultry.

SERVES 4

2 lb/900 g mealy potatoes

4 tbsp butter

3 tbsp hot milk

salt and pepper

INDEX